美国总统演讲系列

REGAN SPEECH SPIRIT EXPLOSION
IN THE GOLDEN AGE

里根演说
黄金时期的精神迸发

任宪宝◎编著

中国言实出版社

图书在版编目（CIP）数据

里根演说：黄金时期的精神迸发：汉英对照 / 任宪宝编．—北京：
中国言实出版社，2014.5

ISBN 978-7-5171-0540-4

Ⅰ．①里… Ⅱ．①任… Ⅲ．①英语－汉语－对照读物 ②里根，
R．（1911～2004）－演讲－汇编 Ⅳ．① H319.4：D

中国版本图书馆 CIP 数据核字（2014）第 083200 号

责任编辑：陈昌财

出版发行 中国言实出版社
地　址：北京市朝阳区北苑路 180 号加利大厦 5 号楼 105 室
邮　编：100101
编辑部：北京市西城区百万庄路甲 16 号五层
邮　编：100037
电　话：61034853（总编室）　　64924716（发行部）
网　址：www.zgyscbs.cn
E-mail：yanshicbs@126.com
经　销 新华书店
印　刷 北京市玖仁伟业印刷有限公司
版　次 2014 年 8 月第 1 版　　2014 年 8 月第 1 次印刷
规　格 787 毫米 ×1092 毫米　　1/16　　印张 15.25
字　数 195 千字
定　价 30.00 元　　　　　ISBN 978-7-5171-0540-4

出版说明

　　自 1776 年《独立宣言》发表至今，美国建国已有两百三十多年。在这一历史阶段中，先后产生了四十四任总统。作为总统共和制国家的美国，其总统兼国家元首和政府首脑双重身份于一身，其在三权分立的国家政治架构中拥有极大的权力和影响力，在国家政治生活中拥有举足轻重的地位。正如美国第二十六任总统西奥多·罗斯福所说，美国总统是"国王和总理大臣的统一体"。

　　在美国，演讲是任何一个准备从政的人士必须具备的基本技能。无论地方议会议员、地方行政首脑还是美国联邦国会议员乃至美国总统，都是通过以演讲为基本形式的竞选活动产生的，这就决定了演讲这种活动在美国政治生活中的重大意义。而作为国家最高领导人的美国总统，他们的演讲往往在表明个人政治见解和基本立场、展露自身意志品质和性格特点的同时，在某种程度上还代表了美国的制度设计与价值观念、反映了美国的文化背景与社会演变。他们的演讲大都是针对当时美国所面临的国内外重大问题，讨论国家内政外交政策的优劣得失，表明解决问题的态度，指出今后的施政方向，激励和动员美国人民克服困难、奋力前行。从美国总统的演讲中，我们可以看到他们对时代潮流的认识、把握和对国家意志的充分表达，可以看到他们的政治才华和不同的人格魅力，还可以看到美国在其国家发展所经历的一个又一个时代转折点上，怎样面对困难、迎接挑战、坚韧不拔，一步步走向成功与成熟。

美国总统的演讲事先大多经过了精心的准备，语言精炼、用词规范、措辞讲究、逻辑严密，不但文采斐然、优美动人，而且有的放矢、言之有物。同时，每个总统的演讲都具有鲜明的个性特色。有的晓之以理，发人深省；有的动之以情，感人肺腑；有的则充满思辨，促使人们对人生、社会乃至世界进行更深层次的思考。

《美国总统演讲系列》丛书，重点选取了美国自成立以来几位重要总统的演讲，其中既有他们的就职演讲、卸任演讲，也有他们在重大事件发生时发表的演讲以及针对一些特定案例向公众发表的演讲等。选取这些演讲，并不代表我们认同其所包含的思想倾向或价值取向，只是想帮助广大读者从这些演讲中，加深对美国国情、美国社会的了解。相信广大读者在对这些演讲进行欣赏的同时，一定会对其反映出的世界观、价值观等做出正确的分析和判断。

编　者

2014 年 5 月

罗纳德·里根是美国第四十任总统。他在走入政坛之前，在社会上奋斗了几十年，并从事过众多行业。这些行业里积累的丰富经验为里根的总统生涯奠定了基础。里根担任过运动广播员、救生员、报社专栏作家、电影演员、电视节目演员和励志讲师，并且是美国影视演员协会的领导人。他的演说风格高明而极具说服力，被媒体誉为"伟大的沟通者"。里根于1967年至1975年担任第三十三任加利福尼亚州州长，1981年到1989年担任总统。

1911年2月6日，里根出生于美国伊利诺伊州坦皮科城。里根父亲的曾祖父迈克尔·里根，于19世纪60年代自爱尔兰移民到美国。他母亲的曾祖父约翰·威尔逊，则是在19世纪40年代从苏格兰移民到美国。里根的父亲约翰·里根是一名信奉天主教的爱尔兰后裔，母亲妮尔·威尔逊是苏格兰、爱尔兰及英国的后裔。

里根最初在狄克森的罗克河畔做救生员。这份工作让他享受扮演救世主的角色，据说他在长达七年的工作中，拯救了七十七名溺水

者。后来里根还开玩笑说，这些溺水者都没有向他道过谢。里根对这段成就相当自豪，常向白宫的访客们展示挂在总统办公室里的罗克河照片。

里根毕业于伊利诺伊州的尤里卡学院，主修经济学和社会学。他极有语言与表演的天赋，这让他在大学里有了充分的用武之地。身为学院新生的他被选为学生罢课的新生演讲人，加入了一次反对减缩学院开支的罢课。1929 年里根加入了兄弟会，后来他认为加入兄弟会的这段经验是学院生涯里最难忘的回忆。他很少花时间在课业上，只拿到了中等的成绩，但他却是校园里许多俱乐部和运动队伍的领导人，被称为"校园里的大角色"。

1932 年，里根先后在爱荷华州的 WOC 广播电台和 WHO 广播电台担任运动播报员，负责播报芝加哥杯棒球赛。他仅凭借球场收报机传来的文字讯息，在广播室里以丰富的想象力来报导比赛进行的情况。有一次比赛进行到第九局时收报线突然故障，但里根仍流畅地虚构比赛进行的情况，直到收报线修复为止。

毕业后里根依然发挥着自己的优势，从事播报行业。1937 年，里根担任芝加哥杯进行前的棒球春训播报员，里根清晰的嗓音、逍遥自在的风格和运动家健硕的体格，使他很受观众欢迎。对他而言，这正是发挥才能之地。后来他只进行了一次试镜，便获得在华纳兄弟公司七年的契约，从而走上了演员的道路。他担任的角色大多是 B 级片里的男主角。就演员职业而言，里根是一个高产的演员。到 1939 年年底，他已经在十九部电影里出演过各种角色。在《克努特·罗克尼》中他饰演足球队员乔治·格里佩，由于一句著名的台词："去替格里佩赢一球！"而获得"格里佩"这个伴随他一生的昵称。里根自认为最好的演出是在 1942 年的《金石盟》里，饰演一名被截肢的年轻人。

后来他还使用里面的台词："我的其余部分在哪里？"作为他自传的书名。

里根在进入政坛之前，曾于 1935 年被任命为美国陆军的后备军官，并在 1941 年 11 月被召集，但由于眼睛患有散光而没有成为第一线战斗人员。而这恰恰为里根发挥自己的才能提供了机会。在珍珠港事件后，里根中尉被分派至陆军航空队的电影小组，制作用于训练和教育的影片，以充分发挥他的演戏才能。他一直待在好莱坞直到战争结束。

1966 年，里根开始参加州长竞选，并一举击败连任两届的派特•布朗，当选了第三十三任加利福尼亚州州长。里根于 1967 年 1 月 3 日宣誓就任加州州长，他在第一届任期中，停止政府雇用更多人员，但也批准提升税率以支撑预算。里根对当时反越战的抗议活动采取强硬路线。1969 年，里根直接派遣了 2,200 名国民警卫队前往镇压在柏克莱加州大学校区的人民公园进行的抗议活动。

1968 年，里根首次参与共和党总统候选人提名，却不幸失败。1976 年，他再次参与提名，对手是时任总统的杰拉尔德•福特，这次提名选举是里根政治生涯中重要的一刻，里根再次以全国代表大会中微弱的票数落败。在全国代表大会上里根发表演说，详尽地阐述了核战争的危险以及苏联在道德上的威胁。他的演说结束后，许多人表示"很后悔投错了票"。

1980 年的总统竞选中，里根在电视辩论上的表现也提升了他的民众形象，他以精湛的辩论技术、优秀的外表和丰富的经验，让自己在电视辩论中获得了极大的优势。选举的结果是里根在普选上获得 43,903,230 票，比卡特的 35,480,115 票高出了 10%。而在选举人票上里根则获得了压倒性的胜利，囊括 489 张选举人票，卡特则只获得 49

张。同时那年的选举还使共和党在参议院中一举增加了 12 个席次，成为参议院的多数党，倒转了二十八年来民主党在参议院保有的多数地位。

在竞选连任的 1984 年美国总统选举中，里根以压倒性胜利击败华特·蒙岱尔，赢得了五十个州里的四十九个州的支持（蒙岱尔只取得他的老家明尼苏达州和华盛顿特区）。里根获得将近 60% 的选票。里根赢得连任的机会一直相当稳固，蒙岱尔在民主党全国代表大会上发表的演说被视为失误连连，在演说中他说道："里根会提升税率，而我也会这样做。但他不会告诉你，而我会。"

里根是第一位亲自揭幕夏季奥运的美国总统。在德州的达拉斯他接受了共和党的提名，借着当时美国经济的复苏而支持度高涨，他在当年夏天亲自揭幕了洛杉矶奥运会。

1984 年的总统竞选中里根做出他最著名的宣战玩笑。他在电台准备发表演说，没有察觉到播音已经开始而开玩笑道："我亲爱的美国人民，我很高兴地告诉你们，今天我签署了一项法案，将会宣布俄国永远为非法状态，我们在五分钟后开始轰炸。"一些人认为在美苏处于如此紧张的状态下发表这种言论是一个大错误。一些人则引用里根的话来质疑里根在外交政策和国际关系上的现实认知。其他人则认为这不过是在录音室里意外流出的一个幽默笑话罢了。这段录音后来还被乐手杰里·哈里森和布特斯·柯林斯改编为舞曲"五分钟"。

尽管在第一场辩论中里根表现不佳，但他在第二场辩论中恢复了优势，并且在整场选战的大多数时候都占据民调的优先位置。里根在 1984 年选战的大胜利，被许多政治评论者认为是"里根式民主"转变了传统民主党支持者的立场所造成的。

当里根就任时，美国经济面临两位数的通货膨胀（将使经济计划相当难以预料）以及 20% 的银行利率（使大多数人难以抵押贷款），将近八百万人处于失业状态。劳工的平均时薪比起五年前下降了 5%，而联邦政府征收的个人税率则平均高达 67%。国债则将近 1 万亿美元。里根在经济上被视为是自由意志主义者，他主张减税、缩小政府规模、减少对商业的管制，但当时没有人清楚他要如何进行，也不确定由民主党占多数的众议院会不会支持他。

除了经济压力外，社会环境还动荡不安。1981 年的夏季，联邦政府机场的大量航管人员由于薪资问题和工作环境的争议，由飞航管制员工会领导发起了违法的罢工。里根依照事先声明的警告，开除了所有参与罢工的航管人员。由于这个工会是 1980 年大选中，少数支持里根的两个工会当中的一个，里根的这个举动在政治上引起了轩然大波。

里根第一届任期的主要目标便是复苏美国的经济，当时美国经济处于所谓的滞胀（停滞的经济发展和高通货膨胀）。里根所下的第一道命令是停止政府对石油价格的控制，以恢复国内在石油生产和探测上的市场动力。为了解决两位数的通货膨胀，里根支持了联邦储备系统主席保罗·沃尔克以戏剧性的效果，提升银行利率来达成减缩货币供应量目标的计划。经济学家米尔顿·佛利民描述，当时里根了解到"若要成功遏止通货膨胀，金融的管制和短暂的经济衰退是不可避免的"。里根利用紧缩货币供应配合全面减税的方法来刺激商业的投资（依据里根的说法："芝加哥经济学派、供应面经济学，随便人们怎么称呼。我注意到有些人甚至称它为里根经济学，直到它开始生效为止……"）。里根的对手嘲笑这是"巫毒经济""涓滴效应"和"里根经济学"，但里根成功地开展全面减税。

为了终结通货膨胀而紧缩货币的供应，使美国经济在 1981 年

7月开始急剧衰退，并在1982年11月降到谷底。美国经济在历经1981~1982年的衰退后，于1983年开始戏剧性的经济复苏，里根政府主张减税帮助了经济的复苏，制造了更多的工作机会，最终使联邦政府获得更多的税收，从20世纪80年代初的每年5,170亿美元大幅提升至1万多亿美元。而里根政府新的军事战略增加了大量军事预算，导致联邦政府的预算赤字达到前所未见的地步。一些批评家则认为，这种将预算大幅投注军事产业的政策，事实上属于古典的凯因斯经济学，并认为接踵而来的经济成长并非减税造成的，而是政府大幅度支出的结果。

当时由民主党占多数的众议院，反对里根如此减缩社会福利和其他国内的支出。由于警觉到社会福利开支的增长，里根指派了阿伦·格林斯潘领导社会福利改革，拟出了减缓社会福利支出的计划。随着年龄的增长，从社会福利取得的津贴也会随之缓慢增长（也配合着逐渐增长的国民平均寿命），使这套制度在接下来的50~70年内不会超出政府的负担能力。这套计划也借着提升社会福利的工资税比率来增加政府的税收。

为了解决预算赤字，里根政府大量由国内和国外贷款国债。到里根第二届任期时，民间所持有的国债已经从1980年占GDP的26%大幅提升至1989年的41%，是自1963年以来最高的纪录。1988年国债总计2.6万亿美元，向国外的借债总额超过了国内，美国也从原本世界最大的债权国转变为世界最大的借债国。

里根的经济政策拉大了贫富间的差距。然而，在里根的任期内，所有经济阶层的所得都提高了，包括最底层的贫穷人口也提升了6%。而同时最富有的1%美国人则提升了1万亿美元的收入。

里根政府被同性恋权利运动以及其他人批评没有迅速处理当时流

行的艾滋病。白宫在 1982 年 10 月第一次讨论这种疾病，里根则在 1985 年的记者会上第一次公开讨论政府处理这种疾病的措施。

尽管遭受批评，里根在任内支出了 570 亿美元以对抗 HIV 和艾滋病，大多数资金都投注至美国国家卫生院。在 HIV 和艾滋病研究上的资源于 1983 年增加了 450%，1984 年增加了 134%，1985 年增加了 99%，1986 年增加了 148%。1985 年 9 月里根说道："包括 1986 年的预算，我们已经投注超过 5 亿元在艾滋病的研究上，我确定其他医学团体也在同步进行这些研究。我们今年有 1 亿元预算，明年将会有 1.26 亿元，所以这是我们放在第一优先的问题。这场疾病的严重性是毫无疑问的，我们必须找出疾病的原因。"到 1986 年里根已经投注大笔经费在艾滋病的预防和研究上，并宣称艾滋病"是我们在健康与人类服务部的公共卫生上排在第一优先的疾病。"

里根还在另一场有关艾滋病的少见争论里扮演重要角色。美国研究员罗伯特·加罗与法国科学家路克·蒙塔尼埃都宣称是自己发现了人类免疫不全的病毒（HIV），并各自为其命名，这场争论最后终于由里根和法国总统弗朗索瓦·密特朗谈判达成共识，让两人和其团队在名称上都占有同样的功劳。这次事件相当的罕见，忽视了在科学上命名的根据，也是第一次在生物学上的争论竟上升到政治的层面。显然，密特朗和里根意识到两个大国不该为了这个议题而产生争执。

虽然里根的第二届任期最显著的是外交上的政策，但他也主导了许多重要的国内法案。1982 年，里根签署法案使 1965 年的选举权法得以延长二十五年期限——尽管在 1980 年的选战中他曾经反对延期。这项法案保护了盲人、残障者和文盲的投票权。其他重要的法案还包括 1986 年的税赋改革法令和 1988 年的公民自由法案——包含了对二战中被拘留的日裔美国人的赔偿。里根也立法授权对牵扯至贩毒的谋

杀行为判处死刑。

米尔顿·佛利民以里根任内每年联邦公文（记录联邦政府每年发布的法规与管制公文）的数量来说明里根反对政府管制的政策走向。自从 20 世纪 60 年代以来，每位总统每年的联邦公文数都持续增加，但里根上任后发出的联邦公文急剧减少，证明了里根对政府管制的反对态度。联邦公文的数量在里根任内都只维持小幅度增长，直到里根离任为止才又开始大量增加。

里根是第一位主张共产主义将会垮台的领导人。1983 年 3 月 3 日他说道："我相信共产主义是人类历史上可悲而怪异的一页——仍在进行中的最后一页。"当时西方对苏联的主流看法是，苏联新一批的领导人时代即将来临，而西方世界必然要跟他们合作。但里根则主张在苏联正处于严重的经济危机之时，借由切断苏联与西方的科技交流来使这种危机加大。他认为苏联最恶劣的是与人类历史的潮流相背，磨灭其人民的自由和尊严。

美国学者对冷战结束的正统观点是"由于自由和民主的西方国家持续地在军事地位上、意识形态的动力上和经济系统上保持优势，最终导致苏联的投降和冷战的结束。这些因素显露了共产主义在道德上的非法性并突出了其经济上的停滞。"这种观点都能被共和党（强调里根扮演的角色）和民主党（强调杜鲁门、肯尼迪、詹森和卡特长期以来的围堵政策）所接受。这种看法也被东欧国家所广泛接受。波兰团结工会的领导人列赫·瓦文萨在 2004 年时说："当谈到罗纳德·里根时，我必须以我个人的角度来谈他，我们在波兰的人都会以我们的角度来谈论他。为什么？因为我们所得到的自由是他给予的。"西德的总理赫尔穆特·科尔则说："他的出现是这个世界的幸运。在里根呼吁戈尔巴乔夫推倒柏林墙后的两年，柏林墙就真的倒了，而十一个月后德国便统一了。"爱尔兰首相伯蒂·埃亨说:"里根总统是共产主义的坚定抵抗者,他扮演了重要的角色,终结了共产主义以及二战后欧洲的分裂。"1989年成为捷克斯洛伐克总统的瓦茨拉夫·哈维尔说:"他是个保持着坚定原则的人,毫无疑问是他促使了共产主义的垮台。"

里根选择强硬的态度与苏联直接对抗,而不像前几位总统如理查德·尼克松、杰拉尔德·福特、吉米·卡特采取缓和政策。他在苏联已经没有能力投注比美国更多军事预算的情况下,展开了新一波的军备竞赛,努力使冷战在经济上和表面上激烈化。

里根政府以"唯有实力才能获致和平"为名的政策进行大规模扩军,这个名称是为了对照西奥多·罗斯福的强硬外交政策和他的名言:"说话温和,手持大棒。"里根政府新设立的对苏政策以赢得冷战为最终目标,这个战略被命名为 NSDD-32。这个战略概述了里根计划在三个战线对抗苏联:经济上减少苏联获取高科技技术的机会,并减少其资源,包括压低苏联商品在世界市场上的价值;军事上增加美国的军事支出,以巩固美国在谈判上的立场,并迫使苏联转移更多经济资源至军事用途上;处理从阿富汗的反苏联游击队,到波兰的团结工会运动。里根并提出了主动战略防御计划,将之称为"星际大战",是以外太空为基础建立的导弹防御网。这通常被美国以外的国家视为是一种威胁,因为它可能抵销苏联对美国"保证互相毁灭"的能力。理论上将使美国发起核战的第一击,并躲过接下来苏联的反击。由于感受到可能因此失去军备竞赛中的平衡地位以及世界的战略根基,苏联的领导人和人民对于情势越来越沮丧。1986年10月里根与苏联领导人戈尔巴乔夫在冰岛会面,戈尔巴乔夫急切地希望美国取消这种防御性同时也是攻击性的导弹防御网。1990年3月11日,立陶宛在新当

选的维陶塔斯·兰茨贝吉斯总统的领导下宣布脱离苏联独立，其余的苏联加盟国也在1991年陆续宣布独立，由此苏联正式瓦解。玛格利特·撒切尔对此描述道："里根不开一枪便赢得了冷战。"

里根主张美国经济开始复苏，快速电脑化的经济、高科技的技术是主要力量，但苏联在这方面远远落后，甚至连韩国的高科技也超越了它，而且一年比一年落后。里根进一步禁止美国和盟国对苏联输出高科技技术，使苏联处境更为恶劣。有一段时间当石油价位极高时，这种落后由于苏联输出了大量石油而得以掩盖，但这个优势在20世纪80年代初期也丧失了。要和西方国家进行经济竞赛显然必须进行彻底的改革，戈尔巴乔夫开始进行改革，他期望新政策中的开放性和新思维能够重新复兴苏联经济，但这些改革却得不到解决的方法，反而产生更多对苏联体制的不满。里根的大规模扩军行动和强硬的反苏言论，造成苏联在1983年北约的例行演习中产生近乎恐慌的反应。虽然这次核战的危机随着演习结束而迅速平息，但这次演习也显示了里根的强硬态度所可能产生的负面后果。一些历史学家，如贝丝·A·菲舍尔认为这次危机对里根的政策有着深远影响，使他对苏联的态度从直接对抗转变为和睦友好的政策。

尽管里根与苏联签订了限武条约，如中程核子武器条约和裁减战略武器谈判，里根依然进行着星际大战计划，部署外人空为基础建立的导弹防御网，以环绕地球的军事卫星来拦截导弹，使美国在核子大战中不受损伤。批评家认为这项计划是不切实际的，而且还违背了反弹道导弹的条约，支持者则认为这项计划能迫使苏联投入更多无法负担的军事支出。事实上，苏联也曾尝试着自行建立一套类似的系统，或至少同时经由限武条约来减缓与美国间的军事差距。最后苏联在后者上表现得较为成功。由于试图追上美国的军事研究而严重损害了原本已经不稳固的苏联经济，这也被认为是导致苏联垮台的主要原因之一。

1987 年 6 月 12 日，罗纳德·里根访问西柏林时，在柏林墙的勃兰登堡门前发表演说："戈尔巴乔夫先生，推倒这堵墙！"由于里根在表达理念时的口才和具有的独特情感而被誉为"伟大的沟通者"。这些口才技巧来自于他担任演员、电视和广播节目主持人以及政治家时逐渐培养的经验，同时身为总统也雇用了技巧高明的演讲稿撰稿者以进一步发挥他的魅力。里根的修辞技巧是相当多变的，他运用强烈甚至是意识形态的言词来指责苏联和共产主义，尤其是在第一届任期时。

但他也能唤起人们将美国视为自由捍卫者的印象和观念。他于 1964 年 11 月 27 日的演讲中将演讲题目取名为"决择的时刻"，重新引入了富兰克林·德拉诺·罗斯福广为人知的著名用词"命运的结合"。其他演讲中他称美国为"山巅上的光辉城市"，称美国人为"慷慨大方、具有理想、大胆勇敢、正派和诚实"的市民并且拥有"梦想英雄目标的权利"。

1986 年 1 月 28 日，在得悉挑战者号意外坠毁后，他延迟了新年国情咨文演说并改向全国发表演说，在演说中他形容那些罹难的宇航员："我们永远不会忘记他们，这也不会是我们最后一次看到他们。因为就在今天早上，他们准备出发并且向我们挥手道别，摆脱了阴沉大地的束缚，而触摸了上帝的脸庞。"（里根引用了美国诗人约翰·吉莱斯皮·玛吉的著名诗句）

里根很幽默，尤其是他的俏皮话，不仅消除了对手的力量，还使他广受大众喜爱。在 1984 年总统选战与华特·蒙岱尔的电视辩论中，在讨论到他的年纪时他妙语道："我不会以我的年纪来作为选

战的议题。我不会以此作为政治目的，来彰显我的对手年幼和缺乏经验。"谈到他的职业时他开玩笑道："政治不是什么糟糕的职业。如果你成功了将会获得许多奖励，如果你可耻的失败了，那你也可以出版一本书。"

里根的支持者和反对者都注意到他开朗乐观的态度，使他比前几任总统更受欢迎。里根有一次如此说道："领导者的教训是相同的，要辛勤地工作，了解事情的真相，乐于倾听并了解他人，坚强的责任感和指挥感，并替你所代表的人民做出最好的决定。"

1981 年 3 月 30 日，刚就任总统六十九天的里根，前往华盛顿特区的希尔顿饭店与美国劳工联合会—产业工会联合会的代表们共进午餐并发表演说。当里根和幕僚们走出饭店大门时，埋伏在饭店门口媒体人潮里的精神病患者欣克利，以一把 22 毫米口径的左轮手枪朝里根射击了六枪，中弹的除了里根外还有白宫新闻秘书和保镖等三人，里根迅速被送至附近的华盛顿大学医院进行紧急手术。

一发子弹击中了里根的腋下，距离心脏只有 1 英寸，里根也因此得以幸免。手术进行时里根还向医生开玩笑道："我希望你们都是共和党人。"（虽然医生并不是，但他仍回复道："我们今天都会支持共和党的。"）当第一夫人南希·里根到达医院时，里根则以重量级拳击冠军杰克·登普西被击倒时的名言向她开玩笑道："亲爱的，我忘记低头了。"

里根的个人魅力使他几乎发表任何言论都能让大众接受，因此而获得了"铁弗龙总统"的绰号。他于伊朗门事件中否认他知情这项交易，但现在存于档案库的国防部长卡斯帕·温伯格的引证则显示出里根知情，这可能是违反了美国宪法的，但他带给公众的形象却是"伟大、坚强的里根冒险以武器来交换人质的自由"。在 1985

年12月里根写了一份秘密的总统"调查"来记载这次"以武器换人质"的计划。里根时代的秘密文件本来可以从 2001 年开始被公开，但乔治·沃克·布什总统签署了一项法案使这些文件将继续无限期保密，从而使人们无法得知更多这方面的资讯。

里根的金融和减税政策被批评拉大了贫富间的差距，他缩减社会福利和所得税率则被一些批评家批评为是加惠富裕人口的政策。在他任内，空前的国债成长也被批评将会危及国家经济的健全。在 20 世纪 80 年代解除了对银行产业的管制后，信用合作社得以自由地将存款人的存款投资至商业不动产上（之前他们被限制只能投资住宅不动产），许多信用合作社开始进行风险性的投资。主掌联邦对产业管制的联邦房屋贷款银行试图限制这种风险行为，于是开始和里根政府的政策产生冲突，里根希望对大多数产业撤销管制——包括银行产业在内。里根也因此拒绝向国会递交联邦房屋贷款银行的预算审核，这项冲突使美国损失了 1,500 亿元，而且几乎导致了信用合作社产业的崩溃。

自由派也批评里根强硬外交政策可能导致核子大战的危机。批评家指出里根忽略了在中南美洲和南非的人权问题，里根对于南非种族隔离制度的支持也被非裔美国人强烈批评。虽然里根也试图结束南非的种族隔离制度并实行自由化，但他反对向南非实行经济上的制裁，认为那是表面上看似有益的制裁计划，事实上将会缩减南非政府的影响力，并让许多南非的好人承受经济的困境。

虽然里根成年后很少出席教堂举办的活动，但他自幼便是一名基督徒，而且时常向基督教团体发表演说。1978 年 3 月里根给一名卫理宗神职人员写了封信，这名神职人员对尼西亚信经持怀疑态度，并指责里根是"主日学校层次的神学"——里根坚定地支持尼西亚信经，并引用了克利夫·史戴普·路易斯的三难困境。不过在里根的国葬上

并没有依照他的信仰和愿望来进行，而是进行了多种信仰的仪式。

1989年1月11日，里根在白宫的总统办公室经由电视转播发表了全国性的告别演说，九天后便离开总统职位，由布什接任。在布什的就职典礼结束后，里根回到了他位于加州圣巴巴拉市附近的大牧场，在那里写自传、骑马、伐木。最后他迁至位于加州贝艾尔的新家。

里根偶尔会代表共和党露面，包括在1992年的共和党全国代表大会上发表了精彩演说。他公开支持单项否决权、平衡预算的宪法修正案和撤销宪法第22号修正案——限制总统只能连任一次的修正案。

几年后里根宣布他被诊断出罹患阿兹海默症。他经由手写信件来向全国说明他的健康状况，由于他一向乐观的态度，他最后总结道："我知道我正在走向我人生旅程中的黄昏。我知道对美国而言前方总是有着灿烂的黎明。谢谢你们，我的朋友们。愿上帝永远祝福你们。"阿兹海默症慢慢地摧毁了里根的脑部能力，迫使他过着与世隔绝的生活。2000年8月，美国《新闻和世界周刊》报道里根病危的消息，但顽强的生命力使里根又活了近四年。到了2003年底，里根进入阿兹海默症的晚期。

2004年6月5日，里根于家中辞世，享年九十三岁。他的遗体也开放让公众瞻仰仪容。整场国葬庄严隆重，在世的数位美国总统和众多外国元首都参加了葬礼。

盖洛普民意测验对美国民众做了一次谁是最受欢迎的美国总统的调查，罗纳德·里根以87%的支持率排名第一。里根在接下来每年的许多民调测验中，继续被选为最好的美国总统之一。同时里根是目前为止活得最久的美国总统。这位总统在有生之年带领美国走出了经济低迷，走出了民主困境，使美国进入了黄金发展时期。

目 录
Contents

第一章

开创国家复兴的时代

第一节 背景介绍

里根于 1966 年踏入政坛，当选第三十三任加利福尼亚州州长。他连续击败连任两届的派特·布朗，并在 1970 年的选战中成功连任。在他第一届任期中，他停止政府雇用更多人员，但也批准提升税率以支撑预算。里根对当时反越战的抗议活动采取强硬路线。1969 年，里根直接派遣了 2,200 名国民警卫队前往镇压，在柏克莱加州大学校区人民公园进行的抗议活动。

1971 年，里根着手改革加州的社会福利。稍早里根曾反对 1964 年的民权法案和 1965 年的民权法案投票。但后来他改变了立场，并认为如果必要的话，民权法案必须动用军事力量来执法。里根也反对建立更大的联邦水坝，以免水坝会淹没溪谷的印地安人农场。他曾和家人一同进行夏季登山，前往内华达山脉考察一处被提议建造高速公路的地点，考察后他便宣布放弃建造的计划。

在死刑的议题上，他强烈支持维持死刑，加州最高法院却在判决中使 1972 年以前加州的死刑宣判全部无效，尽管这个判决后来被宪法修正案所推翻，但这次判决成为里根任内最大的挫折。尽管里根支持死刑，但他在任内颁布了两次赦免和缓刑命令，在里根之后再没有加州州长如此赦免死刑囚犯。里根任内唯一一次执行死刑是在 1967 年 4 月 12 日，从那次以后直到 1992 年为止，加州都没有再执行过死刑。

里根任内还废除了公共的精神病医院系统，改以社区为基础的住宅及医疗来取代非自愿的强制住院，因为他认为那是违反公民的自由。不过从里根任内直到其他的继任者，这种以社区为基础的设施一直都没有充分实现过。

1968 年，里根首次参与共和党总统候选人提名的选举，却没有成功。1976 年，他再次参与提名，对手是时任的杰拉尔德·福特，这次提名选举是里根政治生涯中重要的一刻，杰拉尔德·福特被视为当时共和党内的元老，在全国代表大会中里根再次以几票之差落败。在全国代表大会上里根发表演说，阐述核子战争的危险及苏联在道德上的威胁，听完他动人的演说，许多人表示"很后悔投错了票"。

里根在电视辩论上的表现也提升了他的选情，辩论中他看起来比卡特更为自在。当时正是美国通货膨胀和银行利率急速高涨的时期，在回答观众的问题时他做了非常有力的回答："你觉得你现在的生活比四年前要好吗？"

选举的结果里根在普选上获得 43,903,230 票，比卡特的 35,480,115 票高出了 10%。而在选举人票上里根则获得压倒性胜利，囊括 489 张选举人票，卡特则只获得 49 张。同时那年的选举还使共和党在参议院一举增加了 12 个席次，成为参议院的多数党，倒转了二十八年来民主党在参议院保有多数的地位。

第二节 里根于 1981 年第一次总统就职演讲

Tuesday, January 20, 1981

Senator Hatfield, Mr. Chief Justice, Mr. President, Vice President Bush, Vice President Mondale, Senator Baker, Speaker O'Neill, Reverend Moomaw, and my fellow citizens:

To a few of us here today, this is a solemn and most momentous occasion; and yet, in the history of our Nation, it is a commonplace occurrence. The orderly transfer of authority as called for in the Constitution routinely takes place as it has for almost two centuries and few of us stop to think how unique we really are. In the eyes of many in the world, this every-4-year ceremony we accept as normal is nothing less than a miracle.

Mr. President, I want our fellow citizens to know how much you did to carry on this tradition. By your gracious cooperation in the transition process, you have shown a watching world that we are a united people pledged to maintaining a political system, which guarantees individual liberty to a greater degree than any other, and I thank you, and your people for all your help in maintaining the continuity, which is the bulwark of our Republic.

The business of our nation goes forward. These United States are confronted with an economic affliction of great proportions. We suffer from the longest and one of the worst sustained inflations in our national history. It distorts our economic decisions, penalizes thrift, and crushes the struggling young and the fixed– income elderly alike. It threatens to shatter the lives of millions of our people.

Idle industries have cast workers into unemployment, causing human misery and personal indignity. Those who do work are denied a fair return for their labor by a tax system which penalizes successful achievement and keeps us from maintaining full productivity.

But great as our tax burden is, it has not kept pace with public spending. For decades, we have piled deficit upon deficit, mortgaging our future and our children's future for the temporary convenience of the present. To continue this long trend is to guarantee tremendous social, cultural, political, and economic upheavals.

You and I, as individuals, can, by borrowing, live beyond our means, but for only a limited period of time. Why, then, should we think that collectively, as a nation, we are not bound by that same limitation?

We must act today in order to preserve tomorrow. And let there be no misunderstanding—we are going to begin to act, beginning today.

The economic ills we suffer have come upon us over several decades. They will not go away in days, weeks, or months, but they

will go away. They will go away because we, as Americans, have the capacity now, as we have had in the past, to do whatever needs to be done to preserve this last and greatest bastion of freedom.

In this present crisis, government is not the solution to our problem; government is the problem.

From time to time, we have been tempted to believe that society has become too complex to be managed by self-rule, that government by an elite group is superior to government for, by, and of the people. However, if no one among us is capable of governing himself, then who among us has the capacity to govern someone else?

All of us together, in and out of government, must bear the burden. The solutions we seek must be equitable, with no one group singled out to pay a higher price.

We hear much of special interest groups. Our concern must be for a special interest group that has been too long neglected. It knows no sectional boundaries or ethnic and racial divisions, and it crosses political party lines. It is made up of men and women who raise our food, patrol our streets, man our mines and our factories, teach our children, keep our homes, and heal us when we are sick— professionals, industrialists, shopkeepers, clerks, cabbies, and truck drivers. They are, in short, "We the people," this breed called Americans.

Well, this administration's objective will be a healthy, vigorous, growing economy that provides equal opportunity for all Americans, with no barriers born of bigotry or discrimination. Putting America back to work means putting all Americans back to work. Ending inflation means freeing all Americans from the terror of runaway living costs.

All must share in the productive work of this "new beginning" and all must share in the bounty of a revived economy. With the idealism and fair play, which is the core of our system and our strength, we can have a strong and prosperous America at peace with itself and the world.

So, as we begin, let us take inventory. We are a nation that has a government—not the other way around. Moreover, this makes us special among the nations of the Earth. Our Government has no power except that granted it by the people. It is time to check and reverse the growth of government, which shows signs of having grown beyond the consent of the governed.

It is my intention to curb the size and influence of the Federal establishment and to demand recognition of the distinction between the powers granted to the Federal Government and those reserved to the States or to the people. All of us need to be reminded that the Federal Government did not create the States; the States created the Federal Government.

Now, so there will be no misunderstanding, it is not my intention to do away with government. It is, rather, to make it work—work with us, not over us; to stand by our side, not ride on our back. Government can and must provide opportunity, not smother it; foster productivity, not stifle it.

If we look to the answer as to why, for so many years, we achieved so much, prospered as no other people on Earth, it was because here, in this land, we unleashed the energy and individual genius of man to a greater extent than has ever been done before. Freedom and the dignity of the individual have been more available

and assured here than in any other place on Earth. The price for this freedom at times has been high, but we have never been unwilling to pay that price.

It is no coincidence that our present troubles parallel and are proportionate to the intervention and intrusion in our lives that result from unnecessary and excessive growth of government. It is time for us to realize that we are too great a nation to limit ourselves to small dreams. We are not, as some would have us believe, loomed to an inevitable decline. I do not believe in a fate that will all on us no matter what we do. I do believe in a fate that will fall on us if we do nothing.

So, with all the creative energy at our command, let us begin an era of national renewal. Let us renew our determination, our courage, and our strength. And let us renew; our faith and our hope.

We have every right to dream heroic dreams. Those who say that we are in a time when there are no heroes just don't know where to look. You can see heroes every day going in and out of factory gates. Others, a handful in number, produce enough food to feed all of us and then the world beyond. You meet heroes across a counter—and they are on both sides of that counter. There are entrepreneurs with faith in them and faith in an idea who create new jobs, new wealth and opportunity. They are individuals and families whose taxes support the Government and whose voluntary gifts support church, charity, culture, art, and education. Their patriotism is quiet but deep. Their values sustain our national life.

I have used the words "they" and "their" in speaking of these heroes. I could say "you" and "your" because I am addressing the heroes of whom I speak—you, the citizens of this blessed land.

Your dreams, your hopes, your goals are going to be the dreams, the hopes, and the goals of this administration, so help me God.

We shall reflect the compassion that is so much a part of your makeup. How can we love our country and not love our countrymen, and loving them, reach out a hand when they fall, heal them when they are sick, and provide opportunities to make them self-sufficient so they will be equal in fact and not just in theory?

Can we solve the problems confronting us? Well, the answer is an unequivocal and emphatic "yes". To paraphrase Winston Churchill, I did not take the oath I have just taken with the intention of presiding over the dissolution of the world's strongest economy.

In the days ahead, I will propose removing the roadblocks that have slowed our economy and reduced productivity. Steps will be taken aimed at restoring the balance between the various levels of government. Progress may be slow—measured in inches and feet, not miles—but we will progress. Is it time to reawaken this industrial giant, to get government back within its means, and to lighten our punitive tax burden? In addition, these will be our first priorities, and on these principles, there will be no compromise.

On the eve of our struggle for independence a man who might have been one of the greatest among the Founding Fathers, Dr. Joseph Warren, President of the Massachusetts Congress, said to his fellow Americans, "Our country is in danger, but not to be despaired of... On you depend the fortunes of America. You are to decide the important questions upon which rests the happiness and the liberty of millions yet unborn. Act worthy of yourselves."

Well, I believe we, the Americans of today, are ready to act worthy

of ourselves, ready to do what must be done to ensure happiness and liberty for our children, our children's children and ourselves.

In addition, as we renew ourselves here in our own land, we will be seen as having greater strength throughout the world. We will again be the exemplar of freedom and a beacon of hope for those who do not now have freedom.

To those neighbors and allies who share our freedom, we will strengthen our historic ties and assure them of our support and firm commitment. We will match loyalty with loyalty. We will strive for mutually beneficial relations. We will not use our friendship to impose on their sovereignty, for or own sovereignty is not for sale.

As for the enemies of freedom, those who are potential adversaries, they will be reminded that peace is the highest aspiration of the American people. We will negotiate for it, sacrifice for it; we will not surrender for it—now or ever.

Our forbearance should never be misunderstood. Our reluctance for conflict should not be misjudged as a failure of will. When action is required to preserve our national security, we will act. We will maintain sufficient strength to prevail if need be, knowing that if we do so we have the best chance of never having to use that strength.

Above all, we must realize that no arsenal, or no weapon in the arsenals of the world, is so formidable as the will and moral courage of free men and women. Our adversaries in today's world do not have a weapon. We as Americans do have a weapon. Let that be understood by those who practice terrorism and prey upon their neighbors.

I am told that tens of thousands of prayer meetings are being held on this day, and for that I am deeply grateful. We are a nation under God, and I believe God intended for us to be free. It would be fitting and good, I think, if on each Inauguration Day in future years it should be declared a day of prayer.

This is the first time in history that this ceremony has been held, as you have been told, on this West Front of the Capitol. Standing here, one faces a magnificent vista, opening up on this city's special beauty and history. At the end of this open mall are those shrines to the giants on whose shoulders we stand.

Directly in front of me, the monument to a monumental man: George Washington, Father of our country. A man of humility who came to greatness reluctantly. He led America out of revolutionary victory into infant nationhood. Off to one side, the stately memorial to Thomas Jefferson. *The Declaration of Independence* flames with his eloquence. Then beyond the Reflecting Pool the dignified columns of the Lincoln Memorial. Whoever would understand in his heart the meaning of America will find it in the life of Abraham Lincoln?

Beyond those monuments to heroism is the Potomac River, and on the far shore the sloping hills of Arlington National Cemetery with its row on row of simple white markers bearing crosses or Stars of David. They add up to only a tiny fraction of the price that has been paid for our freedom.

Each one of those markers is a monument to the kinds of hero I spoke of earlier. Their lives ended in places called Belleau Wood, The Argonne, Omaha Beach, Salerno and halfway around the world on Guadalcanal, Tarawa, Pork Chop Hill, the Chosin Reservoir, and in a hundred rice paddies and jungles of a place called Vietnam.

Less than one such marker lays a young man—Martin Treptow—who left his job in a small town barber shop in 1917 to go to France with the famed Rainbow Division. There, on the western front, he was killed trying to carry a message between battalions under heavy artillery fire.

We are told that on his body was found a diary. On the flyleaf under the heading, "My Pledge," he had written these words: "America must win this war. Therefore, I will work, I will save, I will sacrifice, I will endure, and I will fight cheerfully and do my utmost, as if the issue of the whole struggle depended on me alone."

The crisis we are facing today does not require of us the kind of sacrifice that Martin Treptow and so many thousands of others were called upon to make. It does require, however, our best effort, and our willingness to believe in ourselves and to believe in our capacity to perform great deeds; to believe that together, with God's help, we can and will resolve the problems, which now confront us.

In addition, after all, why shouldn't we believe that? We are Americans.

God bless you, and thank you.

1981 年 1 月 20 日，星期二

议员海特菲尔德先生、法官先生、总统先生、副总统布什、蒙代尔先生、议员贝克先生、发言人奥尼尔先生、尊敬的摩麦先生，以及广大支持我的美国同胞们：

今天对于我们大家来说，是一个非常庄严隆重的时刻，对这个国家的历史来说，却是一件普通的事情。按照宪法要求，政府权利正在有序地移交，我们已经如此"例行公事"了两个世纪，很少有人觉得这有什么不妥。但在世界上更多人看来，这个我们已经习以为常的四年一次的仪式，却实在是一个奇迹。

总统先生，我希望我们的国民能够记住你为了这个传承而付出的努力。通过移交程序中的通力合作，你向观察者展示了这样一个事实：我们是发誓要团结起来维护这样一个政治体制的团体，这样的体制保证了我们能够得到比其他政体更为广泛的个人自由。同时我也要感谢你和你的伙伴们的帮助，因为你们坚持了这样的传承，而这恰恰是我们共和国的根基。

我们国家的各项事业都在不断的发展过程中。美国正面临巨大的经济困难。我们遭遇到我国历史上历时最长，最严重的通货膨胀之一，它扰乱着我们的经济决策，打击着节俭的风气，压迫着正在挣扎谋生的青年人和收入固定的中年人，威胁着要摧毁我国千百万人民的生计。

工业发展变缓使工人失业、蒙受痛苦并失去了个人尊严。即使那些有工作的人，也因税收制度的缘故而得不到公正的劳动报酬，因为这种税收制度使我们无法在事业上取得成就，使我们无法保持充分的生产力。

尽管现在我们的纳税负担十分沉重，但还是跟不上公共开支的增长。数十年来，我们的赤字屡屡上升，为图眼前暂时的方便，我们把自己的前途和子孙的前途抵押了出去。这一趋势如果长此以往，必然引起社会、文化、政治和经济等方面的大动荡。

作为独立的个人，你们和我可以靠借贷过一段入不敷出的生活，然而只能维持一段有限的时期，我们怎么可以认为，作为一个国家就不应受到同样的约束呢？

　　为了保住明天，今天我们就必须行动起来。大家都要明白无误地懂得——从今天起我们就要采取行动。

　　几十年来，经济弊病一直袭击着我们，我们深受其害。这些弊病不会在几天、几星期或几个月内消失，但它们终将消失。它们之所以终将消失，是因为作为现在的美国人，我们一如既往地有能力去完成需要完成的事情，以保存这个最后而又最伟大的自由堡垒。

　　在当前这场危机之中，政府的管理不能解决我们面临的问题。政府的管理就是问题所在。

　　我们时常会错误的以为，社会已经越来越复杂，已经不可能凭借自治方式加以管理，而一个由杰出人物组成的政府要比民享、民治、民有的政府高明。可是假如我们之中谁也管理不了自己，那么我们之中谁还能去管理他人呢？

　　不论是政府官员，还是平民百姓，我们必须共同肩负起这个责任，我们谋求的解决办法必须是公平的，不要使任何一个群体付出较高的代价。

　　我们听到许多关于特殊利益集团的谈论，然而，我们必须关心一个被忽视了太久的特殊利益集团。这个集团没有区域之分，没有种族之分，没有民族之分，没有政党之分，这个集团由许许多多的男人与女人组成，他们生产粮食，巡逻街头，管理厂矿，教育儿童，照料家务和治疗疾病。他们是专业人员、实业家、店主、职员、出租汽车司机和货车驾驶员，总而言之，他们就是"我们的人民"，这个称之为美国人的民族。

　　本届政府的目标是必须建立一种健全的、生机勃勃的和不断发展的经济，为全体美国人民提供一种不因偏执或歧视而造成障碍的均等机会，让美国重新工作起来，意味着让全体美国人重新工作起来。制止通货膨胀，意味着让全体美国人从失控的生活费用所造成的恐惧中解脱出来。人人都应分担"新开端"的富有成效的工作，人人都应分享经济复苏的硕果。我国制度和力量的核心是理想主义和公正态度，有了这些我们就能建立起强大、繁荣、国内稳定并同全世界和平相处的美国。

因此，在我们开始改革之际，我们有必要看清现状。我们是一个拥有政府的国家，而不是一个拥有国家的政府。这一点使我们在世界各国中独树一帜，我们的政府除了人民授予的权力，没有任何别的权力。目前，政府权力的膨胀已显示出超过被统治者同意的迹象，制止并扭转这种状况的时候到了。

我打算压缩联邦机构的规模和权力，并要求大家承认联邦政府被授予的权力同各州或人民保留的权利这两者之间的区别。我们大家都需要记住：不是联邦政府创立了各州，而是各州创立了联邦政府。

因此请不要误解，我的意思不是要取消政府，而是要让它发挥作用，同我们一起合作，而不是凌驾于我们之上；同我们并肩而立，而不是骑在我们的背上。政府能够而且必须提供机会，而不是扼杀机会，它能够而且必须促进生产力，而不是抑制生产力。

这么多年来为什么我们能取得这么大的成就，并获得世界上任何一个民族未曾获得的繁荣昌盛，原因就是在这片土地上，我们使人类的能力和个人的才智得到了前所未有的发挥。在这里个人所享有并得以确保的自由和尊严超过了世界上任何其他地方。为这种自由所付出的代价有时相当高昂，但我们从来没有不愿意付出这样的代价。

我们目前的困难是与政府机构因为不必要的过度膨胀而干预、侵扰我们的生活同步增加，这绝不是偶然的巧合。我们是一个决决

大国，不能自囿于小小的梦想，现在正是认识到这一点的时候。我们并非注定走向衰落，尽管有些人想让我们相信这一点。我不相信，无论我们做些什么，我们都将命该如此；但我相信，如果我们什么也不做，我们将的确命该如此。

为此，让我们以掌握的一切创造力来开创一个国家复兴的时代吧。让我们重新拿出决心、勇气和力量，让我们重新建立起我们的信念和希望吧。

我们完全有权去做英雄梦。那些评论我们现在是一个没有英雄时代的人，他们只不过没有用心观察。看啊！每一天进出工厂大门的工人们，辛勤耕作为我们提供食物的农民们，站在柜台后的服务生们，尽心尽力为社会创造财富、提供就业机会的企业家们，交纳赋税以维持国家运作的公民们，所有支持慈善事业、教会、文化及教育的人们，他们的举动是无声的，但爱国心却是不言自明的。他们的价值造就了我们的国家。

我刚才用"他们"这个人称来形容这些英雄，其实我也可以用"你们"。在这个上帝眷顾的国家，你们的梦想，你们的希望，你们的追求就是这个国家存在的理由。

我们的天性包含了同情。倘若我们热爱这个国家，怎么会不热爱自己的同胞。当他们挫折时，扶他们一把；当他们生病时，给予关照。对于弱者给予体面的帮助，使其自立。

我们现在能否战胜摆在面前的问题？答案是明确和肯定的："能！"借用温斯顿·丘吉尔的话："我刚才宣誓并不是想要在我的领导下，使这个世界上最强大的经济瓦解。"

在今后的一段时间，我将提议消除使经济发展缓慢和生产力下降的障碍，采取旨在恢复各级政府之间保持平衡的步骤。进展也许是缓慢的，只能用英寸和英尺来衡量，而不是英里，但我们将一直前进。现在是唤醒工业巨人的时候了，我们首要的任务是减轻惩罚性的赋税负担，使政府能够重新量入为出，在这些原则上绝不会妥协。

在国家立国前夕，我们的建国先贤之一，马塞诸萨州州长约瑟夫·沃伦博士对他的同胞们说："我们的国家正处在危险之中，但我们丝毫不绝望。美国的前途就在我们手中。这个关系到尚未出生的千百万人的幸福和自由的重要问题由你们来决定，你们的行为将无愧于你们自己。"

同胞们，我相信当代的美国人已做好无愧于我们自己人生的准备，做好为确保我们自己、我们的孩子和子孙后代的幸福和自由必须进行行动的准备。

我们庆祝重振美国的此时，全世界的人们都在关注着，我们依旧是那些尚未获得自由的人民心中的自由灯塔！

对于我们的邻居，自由世界的同盟们，我们将进一步加强联络，保证我们承担的义务。我们将以心换心，但我们决不会干涉你们的主权，希望你们也不会干涉我们。

对于自由世界的敌人，我们潜在的对手。我们要使其明白，和平是美国人最高的愿望。我们可以与你们谈判、妥协，但我们决不会屈服，永远不会。

请你们不要误会我们的忍耐，我们努力避免冲突但绝不代表我们屈服。当我们的国家安全受到威胁时，我们会采取行动。我们将保持拥有压倒性对手的武力，因为我们知道只有拥有足够的武力，才能确保我们不会使用武力。

首先，我们必须认识到世界上没有任何武器能比自由人民的道义和勇气更强大。这恰恰是我们美国人民所具备，而我们的对手没

有的武器。这一点，所有支持恐怖主义和觊觎弱小国家者都要明白。

我听说今天各地举行了数以万计的祷告会，我衷心地感到欣慰。我们是上帝护佑的国度，上帝给了我们自由。如果以后每一届的就职日都能成为祷告日，那是很好的事情。

大家都知道，这是历史上第一次在白宫西走廊举行的就职典礼。在这里我们能看到整个首都的风貌，而这广场另一端就是我们先贤们的圣坛。

我的正前方是乔治·华盛顿纪念碑，我们伟大的国父。是他领导了独立革命战争的胜利，并创建了这个国家。在其旁边则是另一位伟大的先贤托马斯·杰弗逊，《独立宣言》的作者。而在水池的尽头是雄伟的林肯纪念堂。从林肯的一生你能体会出什么是美国的精神。

在这些古迹旁是缓缓流淌的波托马可河，而岸边斜斜的山坡正是阿灵顿公墓。这些小小的十字架，六芒星下的墓志铭，述说着我们赢取自由所付出的代价。

每一个墓志铭都是之前我所说的英雄事迹。这些英雄的生命倒在贝洛森林、阿尔贡斤陵、奥马哈海滩、萨勒诺，半个地球外的瓜岛、塔拉瓦岛、长津湖，以及遍地是稻田丛林的叫越南的地方。

在这些墓碑中，有一个叫马丁·特雷普托的年轻人，他在1917年辞掉了小镇理发店的工作，跟随著名的"彩虹师"去了法国，在西线他在为营长传递命令时，被重炮击中而牺牲。

后来，在他的遗体上发现了一本日记。在扉页处他写道："我发誓美国必须赢得这场战争，所以，我会奋斗，我会拯救，我会牺牲，我会忍受，我会奋勇战斗，所有的苦难都将由我一个人来肩负。"

今天我们面临的危机并不要求我们像马丁·特雷普托那样作出如

此巨大的牺牲。但我们也要竭尽全力，有所作为。拥有上帝的协助，我们必能度过危机。

我们有什么理由不相信呢？记住！我们是美国人。

上帝保佑你们，谢谢。

第三节 精彩语录

The economic ills we suffer have come upon us over several decades. They will not go away in days, weeks, or months, but they will go away. They will go away because we, as Americans, have the capacity now, as we have had in the past, to do whatever needs to be done to preserve this last and greatest bastion of freedom.

几十年来，经济弊病一直袭击着我们，我们深受其害。这些弊病不会在几天、几星期或几个月内消失，但它们终将消失。它们之所以终将消失，是因为作为现在的美国人，我们一如既往地有能力去完成需要完成的事情，以保存这个最后而又最伟大的自由堡垒。

All of us together, in and out of government, must bear the burden. The solutions we seek must be equitable, with no one group singled out to pay a higher price.

不论政府官员还是平民百姓，我们必须共同肩负起这个责任，我们谋求的解决办法必须是公平的，不要使任何一个群体付出较高的代价。

This administration's objective will be a healthy, vigorous, growing economy that provides equal opportunity for all Americans, with no barriers born of bigotry or discrimination. Putting America back to work means putting all Americans back to work. Ending inflation means freeing all Americans from the terror of runaway living costs. All must share in the productive work of this "new beginning" and all must share in the bounty of a revived economy. With the idealism and fair play, which is the core of our system and our strength, we can have a strong and prosperous America at peace with itself and the world.

本届政府的目标是必须建立一种健全的、生机勃勃的和不断发展的经济，为全体美国人民提供一种不因偏执或歧视而造成障碍的均等机会，让美国重新工作起来，意味着让全体美国人重新工作起来。制止通货膨胀，意味着让全体美国人从失控的生活费用所造成的恐惧中解脱出来。人人都应分担"新开端"的富有成效的工作，人人都应分享经济复苏的硕果。我国制度和力量的核心是理想主义和公正态度，有了这些我们就能建立起强大、繁荣、国内稳定并同全世界和平相处的美国。

In this land, we unleashed the energy and individual genius of man to a greater extent than has ever been done before. Freedom and the dignity of the individual have been more available and assured here than in any other place on Earth. The price for this freedom at times has

been high, but we have never been unwilling to pay that price.

在这片土地上，我们使人类的能力和个人的才智得到了前所未有的发挥。在这里个人所享有并得以确保的自由和尊严超过了世界上任何其他地方。为这种自由所付出的代价有时相当高昂，但我们从来没有不愿意付出这样的代价。

So, with all the creative energy at our command, let us begin an era of national renewal. Let us renew our determination, our courage, and our strength. In addition, let us renew; our faith and our hope.

为此，让我们以掌握的一切创造力来开创一个国家复兴的时代吧。让我们重新拿出决心、勇气和力量，让我们重新建立起我们的信念和希望吧。

Those who say that we are in a time when there are no heroes just don't know where to look. You can see heroes every day going in and out of factory gates. Others, a handful in number, produce enough food to feed all of us and then the world beyond. You meet heroes across a counter—and they are on both sides of that counter. There are entrepreneurs with faith in themselves and faith in an idea who create new jobs, new wealth and opportunity. They are individuals and families whose taxes support the Government and whose voluntary gifts support church, charity, culture, art, and education. Their patriotism is quiet but deep. Their values sustain our national life.

那些评论我们现在是一个没有英雄时代的人，他们只不过没有用心观察。看啊！每一天进出工厂大门的工人们，辛勤耕作为我们提供食物的农民们，站在柜台后的服务生们，尽心尽力为社会创造财富、提供就业机会的企业家们，交纳赋税以维持国家运作的公民们，所有支持慈善事业、教会、文化及教育的人们，他们的举动是无声的，但爱国心却是不言自明的。他们的价值造就了我们的国家。

I have used the words "they" and "their" in speaking of these heroes. I could say "you" and "your" because I am addressing the heroes of whom I speak—you, the citizens of this blessed land. Your dreams, your hopes, your goals are going to be the dreams, the hopes, and the goals of this administration, so help me God.

我刚才用"他们"这个人称来形容这些英雄，其实我也可以用"你们"。在这个上帝眷顾的国家，你们的梦想，你们的希望，你们的追求就是这个国家存在的理由。

第二章

挣脱大地的束缚

第一节 背景介绍

"挑战者"号航天飞机名字来源于 19 世纪 70 年代航行于大西洋与太平洋上的美国海军的研究船"挑战者"号。

1983 年 4 月 4 日"挑战者"号进行了首次正式发射。在建造之初,其目的是为了作测试用,完成测试任务之后,"挑战者"号被改装成正式的轨道器。在九次飞行行动中,"挑战者"号航天飞机将太空实验室,以及数颗军事和科学卫星送入轨道。1986 年 1 月 28 日,"挑战者"号在执行第十次空间任务时,升空 73 秒后发生爆炸解体坠毁,机上七名宇航员全部遇难。

1986 年 1 月 28 日,在离发射现场 6.4 公里的卡纳维拉尔角看台上,聚集了一千多名观众,其中有十九名中学生代表,他们既是来观看航天飞机发射的,又是来欢送他们的老师麦考利夫。1984 年,航天局宣布将邀请一位教师参加航天飞行,计划在太空为全国中小学生讲授两节有关太空和飞行的科普课,学生们还可以通过专线向麦考利夫提问。麦考利夫是从一万多名教师中挑选出来的。

　　起初，"挑战者"号航天飞机顺利升空，一切正常。飞行 50 秒时，地面曾有人发现航天飞机右侧固体助推器侧部冒出一丝丝白烟，这个现象没有引起人们的注意。52 秒时，地面指挥中心通知指令长斯科比将发动机恢复全速。59 秒时，到达高空 10,000 米，主发动机全速工作，助推器已燃烧了近 450 吨固体燃料。此时，地面控制中心和航天飞机上的计算机显示的各种数据都未见任何异常。65 秒时，斯科比向地面发出最后一句报告词。第 72 秒时，到达高空 16,600 米，航天飞机突然闪出一团亮光，外挂燃料箱凌空爆炸，航天飞机被炸得粉碎，与地面的通讯猝然中断，监控中心屏幕上的数据陡然消失。挑战者号变成了一团大火，两枚失去控制的固体助推火箭脱离火球，成 V 字形喷着火焰向前飞去，即将掉入人口稠密的陆地，航天中心负责安全的军官比林格在第 100 秒时，通过遥控装置将它们引爆。爆炸后的碎片在发射场东南方 30 公里处散落了 1 小时之久，价值 12 亿美元的航天飞机被炸成碎片坠入大西洋。导致爆炸的起因是助推器两个部件之间的接头破损，喷出的燃气烧穿了助推器的外壳，继而引燃外挂燃料箱。燃料箱裂开后，液氢在空气中剧烈燃烧爆炸。

　　"挑战者"号航天飞机上的七名宇航员分别是：机长：弗朗西斯·斯科比，四十六岁；驾驶员：迈克尔·史密斯，四十岁；宇航员：朱迪恩·雷斯尼克（女），三十六岁；罗纳德·麦克奈尔，三十五岁；埃利森·鬼冢，三十九岁；格里高利·杰维斯，四十一岁；教师：克里斯塔·麦考利夫（女），三十七岁。

　　机长弗朗西斯·斯科比曾是美国空军战斗机飞行员。驾驶员迈克尔·史密斯曾在美国海军服役，担任过战斗机飞行员，多次获得奖章，其中包括海军特级飞行十字勋章和国家敢于战斗银星十字勋章。克里斯塔·麦考利夫出生于美国波士顿，在新罕布什尔州康科

德中学任教。

"挑战者"号航天飞机爆炸的消息像冲击波一样传遍了美国各地及全世界。在华盛顿的国会山，国会工作人员、参议员和众议员们聚集在电视机旁，默默地观看着这幕悲剧的发展。政治家们的情感是克制和理性的，因为他们清楚地知道，"挑战者"号的惨剧是航天史上迄今最大的惨祸，但不是第一次，也不会是最后一次。

"挑战者"号航天飞机爆炸后，里根立刻在他的椭圆形办公室发表了谈话，他神情忧郁，语调沉重地说："原计划今晚我将对你们发表讲话，就国情咨文做报告，但是，今天早上发生的事件使我改变了计划。今天是哀悼和纪念之日。"他接着说，"南希和我对'挑战者'号发生的悲剧深感哀痛。我一直十分信任和尊重我们的太空计划，今天所发生的事情决不会降低它的声誉。我们还要继续对太空进行探索。"他宣布说："今后还要进行更多的航天飞行，要有更多的宇航员。太空里要有更多的志愿者，更多的平民，更多的教师。"

在回答记者关于航天飞机计划的前途问题时，斯皮克斯引用里根的话说："这些人都献身于对太空的探索。我们纪念这些勇敢的人的最好办法莫过于继续执行这个计划。"

1月28日当天，联合国和许多国家的领导人纷纷发表讲话或致电里根总统，对"挑战者"号不幸失事表示同情和哀悼。联合国秘书长佩雷斯·德奎利亚尔向里根总统发出了言语切切的唁电："全世界都将为这一开拓人类知识边疆中，悲剧性的牺牲而万分悲痛。"联合国安理会获悉这一消息时正在开会，会议从而中止。联大安理会主席李鹿野代表安理会发表讲话："对美国航天探索中出现的这一机毁人亡事件感到十分悲痛。"

1月28日正午，华盛顿和美国各州下半旗致哀。街道比平时安静了许多，人们都默默赶路一言不发。入夜，灯火辉煌的纽约帝国大厦熄灭了灯火以示哀悼。这个"全美国的灾难"深深地震撼着人们的心灵。

美国原定1986年将进行十五次航天飞机的发射，是太空时代开始后最重要的一年，此时全部化为泡影。建造"挑战者"号航天飞机花费了美国纳税者12亿美元，轰然一声巨响使这笔巨资化为乌有。美国三大电视网，哥伦比亚广播公司、美国广播公司和全国广播公司，在1月28日当天用了五个多小时连续报道"挑战者"号爆炸事件，损失的广告费总额达900万美元。

1986年1月31日，1.5万名航天工作者冒着寒风，在休斯敦约翰逊航天中心，为失事的七名机组人员举行了追悼仪式。里根总统出席追悼仪式并慰问了遇难者家属。

"挑战者"号的事故对美国太空计划的影响难以估量。许多卫星和航天器的发射计划，以及准备在太空中进行的研究项目都将大大推迟，有些不得不取消。其中受影响最大的三个重要航天飞行计划是：原定3月15日由"挑战者"号为欧洲航天局发射的"尤利西斯"航天器，进行绕太阳的南北极飞行。以及定于3月20日和10月由"亚特兰蒂斯"号分别发射的"伽利略"航天器和"哈勃"太空望远镜。"伽利略"航天器计划飞往木星探测，价值12亿美元的"哈勃"太空望远镜则准备送入地球轨道，观测宇宙的"边缘"。由于航天器的发射需要等待行星之间合适的相对位置，错过了时机只能重新等待机会。当时的这种局面已不可避免。当年预期要发射的六颗商业通讯卫星，也因而取消了。

"挑战者"号的爆炸，使同航天飞机飞行计划有关的公司和依

靠航天飞机部署卫星的公司遭遇财政困难，航天飞机的主要制造和维修公司洛克希德飞机公司和罗克韦尔国际公司的股票猛跌。

美国五角大楼在"挑战者"号失事事件中受到的打击最为沉重。如果美国航天局另外定购一架新的航天飞机，那么大约需要17亿美元的费用和五年的光阴。有些国际问题专家认为这次事故可能置"星球大战"计划于"险境"。五角大楼一直利用航天飞行进行战略防御计划的基础实验，苏联十分关心这次事故能否阻止美国实施这一计划。塔斯社说，这场悲剧表明美国的宇航技术是不可靠的。这一事件严重震撼了美国的军事和外交地位。

到此为止，这场惊心动魄的航天悲剧似乎要落幕了，不过正当美国总统调查委员会调查"挑战者"号爆炸的原因时，第一名进入太空的新闻记者已经开始挑选了。设在南卡罗来纳大学的太空记者办事处已经收到了1,703份申请书。由于"挑战者"号的爆炸使这一工作推迟了三周，但没有人因为航天飞机爆炸而撤回申请。

美国众多的宇航员中没有人表示要退出航天生涯，而是希望能在航天飞机恢复飞行后，参加第一次飞行。怀俄明州和纽约州的学生提出倡议，号召全国中小学生每人捐出一美元，用来建造一架新的"挑战者"号。他们的倡议获得了佛罗里达州和缅因州幼儿园儿童的响应。《美国新闻与世界报道》举行的一次民意测验中，大约有三分之二的美国人表示，他们认为航天事业应当继续，他们愿为探测太空事业付出代价。

苏联政府决定，以麦考利夫和另一位遇难的美国女宇航员雷斯尼克的名字，命名金星上的两座环形火山。

美国哈佛大学史密森天体物理研究所所属的哈佛大学小行星研究所决定，将用七名美国宇航员的名字为1980年以来发现的在火星和木星轨道之间绕太阳运行的七颗小行星命名。

"挑战者"号遇难的七名宇航员给人类探索太空奠定了基础。在这些罹难的人中有白人和黑人、男人和女人，甚至还有一位日裔美国人，所以在客观上起到了凝聚美国各民族的作用。"挑战者"号的失事使全人类更深刻地理解了征服太空的艰难历程，从而坚定了走出地球的决心。

第二节 里根于 1986 年悼念 "挑战者" 号 宇航员的演讲

Ladies and Gentlemen, I'd planned to speak to you tonight to report on the state of the Union, but the events of earlier today have led me to change those plans. Today is a day for mourning and remembering. Nancy and I are pained to the core by the tragedy of the shuttle Challenger. We know we share this pain with all of the people of our country. This is truly a national loss.

Nineteen years ago, almost to the day, we lost three astronauts in a terrible accident on the ground. However, we've never lost an astronaut in flight. We've never had a tragedy like this. And perhaps we've forgotten the courage it took for the crew of the shuttle. However, they, the Challenger Seven, were aware of the dangers, but overcame them and did their jobs brilliantly. We mourn seven heroes: Michael Smith, Dick Scobey, Judith Resnik, Ronald McNair, Ellison Onizuka, Gregory Jarvis, and Christa McAuliffe. We mourn their loss as a nation together.

For the families of the seven, we cannot bear, as you do, the full impact of this tragedy. But we feel the loss, and we're thinking about you so very much. Your loved ones were daring and brave, and they had that special grace, that special spirit that says, "Give me a challenge, and I'll meet it with joy." They had a hunger to explore the universe and discover its truths. They wished to serve, and they did. They served all of us.

We've grown used to wonders in this century. It's hard to dazzle us. But for twenty-five years the United States space program has been doing just that. We've grown used to the idea of space, and, perhaps we forget that we've only just begun. We're still pioneers. They, the members of the Challenger crew, were pioneers.

And I want to say something to the schoolchildren of America who were watching the live coverage of the shuttle's take-off. I know it's hard to understand, but sometimes painful things like this happen. It's all part of the process of exploration and discovery. It's all part of taking a chance and expanding man's horizons. The future doesn't belong to the fainthearted; it belongs to the brave. The Challenger crew was pulling us into the future, and we'll continue to follow them.

I've always had great faith in and respect for our space program. In addition, what happened today does nothing to diminish it. We do not hide our space program. We do not keep secrets and cover things up. We do it all up front and in public. That is the way freedom is, and we wouldn't change it for a minute.

We'll continue our quest in space. There will be more shuttle flights and more shuttle crews and, yes, more volunteers, more civilians, more teachers in space. Nothing ends here; our hopes and

our journeys continue.

I want to add that I wish I could talk to every man and woman who works for NASA, or who worked on this mission and tell them: "Your dedication and professionalism have moved and impressed us for decades. And we know of your anguish. We share it."

There's a coincidence today. On this day 390 years ago, the great explorer Sir Francis Drake died aboard ship off the coast of Panama. In his lifetime, the great frontiers were the oceans, and a historian later said, "He lived by the sea, died on it, and was buried in it." Well, today, we can say of the Challenger crew: Their dedication was, like Drake's, complete.

The crew of the space shuttle Challenger honored us by the manner in which they lived their lives. We will never forget them, or the last time we saw them, this morning, as they prepared for their journey, waved goodbye, and "slipped the surly bonds of earth to touch the face of God."

Thank you.

女士们、先生们：本来我打算今天晚上向你们宣读国情咨文，但今天早些时候发生的事件让我改变了计划。今天是哀悼和怀念的日子。南希和我为"挑战者号"航天飞机的悲剧感到至为痛心。我们知道全体国人人同此心。这真是国人的损失。

十九年前，几乎是同一天，在一次可怕的地面事故中，我们丧失了三名宇航员。然而，我们从未在飞行中丧失过宇航员，从未经历过这样的灾难。也许我们已经忘记航天飞机机组人员需要多么大的勇气，但是挑战者七壮士深知其中的危险，他们坚韧不拔，出色地履行了自己的职责。我们悼念七位英雄：迈克尔·史密斯、迪克·斯科比、朱迪恩·伦斯尼克、罗纳德·卖克奈尔、埃利森·奥尼祖卡、格雷戈里·贾维斯、克丽斯塔·麦考利夫。我们举国哀悼失去的英雄。

虽然我们不能像这七名宇航员的家人那样感受这场灾难的打击。但是我们感受到了损失，我们认为你们一定也是如此。你们的亲人勇敢无畏，他们卓越的魅力和人格精神告诉我们："请给予我挑战，我要满怀喜悦的去迎接。"他们渴望探索宇宙，渴望揭开宇宙的奥秘。他们希望尽职，他们做到了。他们为我们所有的人尽了职。

这个世纪我们对奇迹已习以为常，很难有什么会使我们赞叹不已，但是美国航天计划二十五年来做的正是如此。我们对太空计划已经习以为常，也许已经忘了我们不过刚刚起步，我们仍然是开拓者。他们——挑战者号全体机组人员是开拓者。

我要对观看航天飞机发射直播的美国学童说几句话。我知道这件事情令你们难以理解，但有时像这样令人痛苦的事确实会发生。这些都是探索和发现过程的一部分，这些都是承担风险和拓展人类世界范围的一部分。未来不属于弱者，未来属于强者。挑战者号全体人员把我们推向未来，我们将继续追随他们。

我一直对我们的航天计划充满信心并怀抱敬意，今天发生的悲剧决不会削弱它。我们没有隐藏自己的航天计划，我们没有保密和隐瞒，我们堂堂正正地公开实施它。这正是自由的方式，我们一分钟也不会改变它。

我们将继续探索太空。我们将有更多次的航天飞行，有更多的宇航员，更多的志愿者，更多的平民，更多的教师进入太空。一切都不会到此为止。我们的希望和我们的旅程不会停步。

我还想说，但愿我能与每一位为国家航空航天局，或者为完成

此次使命而工作的人谈话，告诉他们："几十年来，你们的奉献和敬业精神令我们感动，让我们铭记在心。我们了解你们的痛苦。我们感同身受。"

今天是一个巧合。三百九十年前的今天，伟大的探险家佛朗西斯·德雷克勋爵在巴拿马附近海面的一条船上逝去。在他生活的时代，最大的疆界就是海洋。后来一位历史学家说："他生在海边，死在海上，葬在海里。"今天对于"挑战者"号宇航员我们可以这样说：像德雷克一样，他们的奉献是毫无保留的。

"挑战者"号航天飞机宇航员的生命历程给我们带来荣耀，我们永远不会忘记他们，也不会忘记今天早上最后一次见到他们，那时他们正准备上路，挥手告别，"挣脱大地坚固的束缚，去触摸上帝的脸"。

谢谢各位。

第三节 精彩语录

We've grown used to wonders in this century. It's hard to dazzle us. But for twenty-five years the United States space program has been doing just that. We've grown used to the idea of space, and, perhaps we forget that we've only just begun. We're still pioneers.

这个世纪我们对奇迹已习以为常，很难有什么会使我们赞叹不已，但是美国航天计划二十五年来做的正是如此。我们对太空计划已经习以为常，也许已经忘了我们不过刚刚起步，我们仍然是开拓者。

It's all part of the process of exploration and discovery. It's all part of taking a chance and expanding man's horizons. The future doesn't belong to the fainthearted; it belongs to the brave. The Challenger crew was pulling us into the future, and we'll continue to follow them.

这些都是探索和发现过程的一部分，这些都是承担风险和拓展人类世界范围的一部分。未来不属于弱者，未来属于强者。挑战者

号全体人员把我们推向未来，我们将继续追随他们。

We'll continue our quest in space. There will be more shuttle flights and more shuttle crews and, yes, more volunteers, more civilians, more teachers in space. Nothing ends here; our hopes and our journeys continue.

我们将继续探索太空。我们将有更多次的航天飞行，有更多的宇航员，更多的志愿者，更多的平民，更多的教师进入太空。一切都不会到此为止。我们的希望和我们的旅程不会停步。

第三章

为持久的友谊奠定基础

第一节 背景介绍

中美关系在近两个世纪渐渐成为了世界热点。历届美国政府对中国的态度也成为了研究的重点。罗纳德·威尔逊·里根是美国历史上最受民众欢迎的总统之一，对中国人而言，里根之名也非常耳熟。里根在任的八年里，中美关系虽然磕磕绊绊，但也得到了长足的发展，延续了两国的"蜜月期"。

里根总统宣誓就职时，中美正式建立正常外交关系才一年，但这位共和党出身的总统似乎对中华人民共和国并不友好，反而对台湾表现出很高的热情。例如，里根在竞选总统前一直以为台湾是中国的合法政府，甚至在竞选时提出了"倒联络处方案"，即参考1973年时，台湾当局在美国设立"大使馆"，中国在美国设联络处的方式。现在已倒过来，让中国在美国设立大使馆，而让台湾在美国设立联络处。

里根当选总统后，还邀请台湾的国民党秘书长蒋彦士出席他的就职典礼，打算允许台湾在美增设"北美事务协调委员会"分支机构。

在对华政策上积极贯彻《对台湾关系法》，向台湾出售防御性武器等。当时，鉴于台湾问题的敏感性，里根的言行无意给脆弱的中美关系蒙上了厚厚的阴霾。

里根的对华态度，加上当时中美两国就美国对台湾销售武器进行的正式会谈以及非正式磋商都陷入僵局，这使中国政府感到非常不满。在此背景下，里根决定派遣他的竞选伙伴、副总统乔治·布什访华。

1982年5月5日至9日，布什访问中国，并与当时的中共中央副主席邓小平会面。邓小平警告说，美国向台湾卖武器问题是中美关系中的一个阴影，而且对今天来说是一个潜伏的危机。如果两国关系中的这个疙瘩能够解开，将对全球战略很有利。而布什也大放好话，称里根政府无意搞"两个中国"。

布什访华的成果是中美关系更进一步。同年8月17日，两国发表了旨在解决美国售台武器问题的《中华人民共和国和美利坚合众国联合公报》（又称《八·一七公报》）。这一公报连同《上海公报》和《中美建交公报》一起，即通常所称的中美三个联合公报，构成中美关系的基础。

但里根对《八·一七公报》并不满意，他认为该公报对美国来说不理想，所以他加了附带条款，即如果美国支持台湾，台湾会对大陆开放，而不会朝独立发展，这是他任内一再暗示的逻辑。

如果说尼克松打开了中美关系的大门，而卡特完成了这一历史进程的话，那么里根在推动中美关系上可谓迈出了一大步。继布什访华后，里根也于1984年4月26日至5月1日对中国进行了国事访问，成为中美建交后首位在任时来华访问的美国总统。对于里根的到访，中国方面自然不会怠慢，国家主席李先念和军委主席邓小

平先后出面接见。

在访华期间，里根参观了西安兵马俑，并到复旦大学发表演讲，让更多的中国人了解了这位美国总统。但更重要的是，在此期间，中美双方签订了《避免双重征税》和《防止偷漏税》等四项协定和议定书，并草签了《中美和平利用核能合作协定》。

里根推动了中美之间的经贸投资关系，让两国共蒙其利。不仅如此，中美的军事交流、经济交流、科学交流和人员往来发展得都比较顺利。因此人们普遍认为，里根时期是中美关系的重要发展期。

第二节 里根于 1984 年在复旦大学的演讲

We have been in your country only 5 days, but already we have seen the wonders of a lifetime—the Great Wall of China, a structure so huge and marvelous that it can be seen from space; the ancient city of Xi'an; and the Tomb of the Great Emperor and the buried army that guards him still. These are the wonders of ages past.

But today I want to talk to you, the young people of a great university, about the future, about our future together and how we can transform human life on this planet if we bring as much wisdom and curiosity to each other as we bring to our scholarly pursuits.

I want to begin, though, with some greetings. I bring you greetings not only from my countrymen but from one of your countrymen. Some of you know Ye Yang, who was a student here. He graduated from Fudan and became a teacher of English at this university. Now he is at Harvard University in the United States, where he is studying for a doctorate in comparative literature.

My staff spoke to him before we left. Mr. Ye wants you to know he is doing fine. He is working hard on his spring term papers, and his thoughts turn to you often. He asked me to deliver a message to his former students, colleagues, friends, and family. He asked me to say for him, and I hope I can, "Wo xiang nian da jia".

He wants you to know that he looks forward to returning to Fudan to teach. And President Xie, he said to tell you he misses your friendship and encouragement. And Mr. Ye says you are a very great woman and a great educator. You will be proud to know that he received straight as last term. And when we congratulated him, he said, "I have nothing to be proud of myself; I am so proud of my university."

I'd like to say a few words about our China-U.S. educational exchange programs. It's not entirely new, this exchanging of students. Your President Xie earned a degree from Smith College in the United States. Smith is also my wife Nancy's alma mater. And President Xie also attended MIT, Massachusetts Institute of Technology, one of our greatest universities of science, engineering, and technology.

But in the past few years, our two countries have enjoyed an explosion in the number of student exchanges. Five years ago, you numbered your students studying abroad in the hundreds. Since then, 20,000 Chinese scholars have studied throughout the world, and more than half of them have come to American schools. More than 100 American colleges and universities now have educational exchanges with nearly as many Chinese institutions.

We have committed more resources to our Fulbright program in China than in any other country. Two of the American professors teaching here at Fudan are Fulbright professors. And there are 20 American students studying with you, and we're very proud of them.

American students come to China to learn many things—how you monitor and predict earthquakes, how you've made such strides in researching the cause and treatment of cancer. We have much to learn from you in neurosurgery and in your use of herbs in medicine. And we welcome the chance to study your language, your history, and your society.

You, in turn, have shown that you're eager to learn, to come to American schools and study electronics and computer sciences, math and engineering, physics, management, and the humanities. We have much to share in these fields, and we're eager to benefit from your curiosity. Much of this sharing is recent, only 5 years old. But the areas of our mutual cooperation continue to expand. We've already agreed to cooperate more closely in trade, technology, investment, and exchanges of scientific and managerial expertise. And we have just concluded an important agreement to help advance our technological and economic development through the peaceful use of nuclear energy.

That term "peaceful use of nuclear energy" is a key. Our agreement rests upon important principles of nonproliferation. Neither of our countries will encourage nuclear proliferation nor assist any other country to acquire or develop any nuclear explosive device.

We live in a troubled world, and the United States and China, as two great nations, share a special responsibility to help reduce the risks of war. We both agree that there can be only one sane policy to preserve our precious civilization in this modern age: A nuclear war

cannot be won and must never be fought. And no matter how great the obstacles may seem, we must never stop our efforts to reduce the weapons of war. We must never stop at all until we see the day when nuclear arms have been banished from the face of this Earth.

With peaceful cooperation as our guide, the possibilities for future progress are great. For example, we look forward to exploring with China the possibilities of cooperating in the development of space on behalf of our fellow citizens.

Our astronauts have found that by working in the zero gravity environment of space, we will be able to manufacture life-saving medicines with far greater purity and efficiency, medicines that will treat diseases of heart attack and stroke that afflict millions of us. We will learn how to manufacture Factor 8, a rare and expensive medicine used to treat hemophiliacs. We can research the Beta Cell, which produces insulin, and which could provide mankind's first permanent cure for diabetes.

New satellites can be launched for use in navigation, weather forecasting, broadcasting, and computer technology. We already have the technology to make the extraordinary commonplace. We hope to see the day when a Chinese scientist working out an engineering problem in Fudan will be able to hook into the help of a scientist at a computer at MIT. And the scientist in Boston will be able to call on the expertise of the scientist in Shanghai, and all of it in a matter of seconds.

My young friends, this is the way of the future. By pooling our talents and resources, we can make space a new frontier of peace.

Your government's policy of forging closer ties in the free

exchange of knowledge has not only enlivened your economy, it has opened the way to a new convergence of Chinese and American interests. You have opened the door, and let me assure you that ours is also open.

Now, all of this is particularly exciting in light of the recent history of our two countries. For many years, there was no closeness between us. The silence took its toll. A dozen years ago, it began to change. Together, we made it change. Now in the past 5 years, your policy of opening to the outside world has helped us begin to know each other better than we ever had before.

But that process has just begun. To many Americans, China is still a faraway place, unknown, unseen, and fascinating. And we are fascinated.

I wonder if you're aware of the many ways China has touched American life. The signs of your influence and success abound. If I were spending this afternoon in Washington, I might look out the window and see a man and woman strolling along Pennsylvania Avenue wearing Chinese silk. They might be on their way to our National Portrait Gallery to see the Chinese art exhibit. And from there, perhaps they would stroll to our National Gallery to see the new building designed by the Chinese American architect, I.M. Pei. After that, they might end their day dining in a restaurant that serves Chinese cuisine.

We associate China with vitality, enormous vitality, and something that doesn't always go along with that—subtlety, the subtlety of discerning and intelligent minds.

Premier Zhao saw something of the American attitude toward

China when he visited us in January. He said after a few days in our country that he never expected such profound feelings of friendship among the American people for the Chinese people.

Well, let me say, I'm happy to return the compliment. I have found the people of China to be just as warm and friendly toward us, and it's made us very glad.

But meeting you and talking to you has only made me want to know more. And I sense that you feel the same way about Americans. You, too, wish to know more.

I would like to tell you something about us, and also share something of my own values.

First of all, America is really many Americas. We call ourselves a nation of immigrants, and that's truly, what we are. We have drawn people from every corner of the Earth. We're composed of virtually every race and religion, and not in small numbers, but large. We have a statue in New York Harbor that speaks of this, a statue of a woman holding a torch of welcome to those who enter our country to become Americans. She has greeted millions upon millions of immigrants to our country. She welcomes them still. She represents our open door.

All of the immigrants who came to us brought their own music, literature, customs, and ideas. And the marvelous thing, a thing of which we're proud, is they did not have to relinquish these things in order to fit in. In fact, what they brought to America became American. And this diversity has more than enriched us; it has literally shaped us.

This tradition—the tradition of new immigrants adding to the sum total of what we are—is not a thing of the past. New immigrants are still bringing their talents and improving the quality of American life. Let me name a few—I think you'll know their names.

In America, Wang computers have become a fixture in offices throughout the country. They are the product of the energy and brilliance of Mr. a Wang, who himself is the product of a Shanghai university.

The faces of our cities shine with the gleaming buildings of Mr. I.M. Pei, who first became interested in architecture as a student here in Shanghai.

What we know of the universe and the fundamental nature of matter has been expanded by the Nobel Prize winning scientist, Dr. Lee Tsung-Dao, who was born in Shanghai.

We admire these men; we honor them; and we salute you for what you gave them that helped make them great.

Sometimes in America, some of our people may disagree with each other. We are often a highly disputatious nation. We rather like to argue. We are free to disagree among ourselves, and we do. But we always hold together as a society. We've held together for more than 200 years, because we're united by certain things in which we all believe, things to which we've quietly pledged our deepest loyalties.

I draw your special attention to what I'm about to say, because it's so important to an understanding of my country.We believe in the dignity of each man, woman, and child. Our entire system is founded on an appreciation of the special genius of each individual, and of his special right to make his own decisions and lead his own life.

We believe—and we believe it so deeply that Americans know

these words by heart—we believe "that all men are created equal, that they are endowed by their Creator with certain unalienable Rights, that among those are Life, Liberty and the pursuit of Happiness." Take an American student or teacher aside later today and ask if he or she hasn't committed those words to memory. They are from the document by which we created our nation, *the Declaration of Independence*.

We elect our government by the vote of the people. That is how we choose our Congress and our President. We say of our country, "Here the People Rule, " and it is so.

Let me tell you something of the American character. You might think that with such a varied nation, there couldn't be one character, but in many fundamental ways, there is.

We are a fair-minded people. We're taught not to take what belongs to others. Many of us, as I said, are the children, grandchildren, and great-grandchildren of immigrants, and from them we learned something of hard labor. As a nation we toiled up from poverty, and no people on Earth are more worthy to be trusted than those who have worked hard for what they have. None is less inclined to take what is not theirs.

We're idealists. Americans love freedom, and we've fought and died to protect the freedom of others. When the armies of fascism swept Europe four decades ago, the American people fought at great cost to defend the countries under assault.

When the armies of fascism swept Asia, we fought with you to stop them. And some of you listening today remember those days, remember when our General Jimmy Doolittle and his squadron came halfway around the world to help. Some of those pilots landed in China. You remember those brave young men. You hid them and cared for them and bound up their wounds. You saved many of their lives.

When the Second World War was won, the United States voluntarily withdrew from the faraway places in which we had fought. We kept no permanent armies of occupation. We didn't take an inch of territory, nor do we occupy one today. Our record of respect for the freedom and independence of others is clear.

We're a compassionate people. When the war ended, we helped rebuild our allies—and our enemies as well. We did this because we wanted to help the innocent victims of bad governments and bad policies, and because, if they prospered, peace would be more secure.

We're an optimistic people. Like you, we inherited a vast land of endless skies, tall mountains, rich fields, and open prairies. It made us see the possibilities in everything. It made us hopeful. And we devised an economic system that rewarded individual effort that gave us good reason for hope.

We love peace. We hate war. We think—and always have—that war is a great sin, a woeful waste. We wish to be at peace with our neighbors. We want to live in harmony with friends.

There is one other part of our national character I wish to speak of. Religion and faith are very important to us. We're a nation of many religions. But most Americans derive their religious belief from the *Bible* of Moses, who delivered a people from slavery; the *Bible* of Jesus Christ, who told us to love thy neighbor as thyself, to do unto your neighbor as you would have him do unto you.

And this, too, has formed us. It's why we wish well for others. It's why it grieves us when we hear of people who cannot live up to their full potential and who cannot live in peace.

We invite you to know us. That is the beginning of friendship between people. And friendship between people is the basis for friendship between governments.

The silence between our governments has ended. In the past 12 years, our people have become reacquainted, and now our relationship is maturing. And we're at the point where we can build the basis for a lasting friendship.

Now, you know, as I do, that there is much that naturally divides us: time and space, different languages and values, different cultures and histories, and political systems that are fundamentally different. It would be foolish not to acknowledge these differences. There's no point in hiding the truth for the sake of a friendship, for a friendship based on fiction will not long withstand the rigors of this world.

But let us, for a moment, put aside the words that name our differences and think what we have in common. We are two great and huge nations on opposite sides of the globe. We are both countries of great vitality and strength. You are the most populous country on Earth; we are the most technologically developed. Each of us holds a special weight in our respective sides of the world.

There exists between us a kind of equipoise. Those of you who are engineering students will perhaps appreciate that term. It speaks of a fine and special balance.

Already there are some political concerns that align us, and there are some important questions on which we both agree. Both the United States and China oppose the brutal and illegal occupation of Kampuchea. Both the United States and China have stood together in condemning the evil and unlawful invasion of Afghanistan. Both the United States and China now share a stake in preserving peace on the Korean Peninsula, and we share a stake in preserving peace in this area of the world.

Neither of us is an expansionist power. We do not desire your land, nor you ours. We do not challenge your borders. We do not provoke your anxieties. In fact, both the United States and China are forced to arm themselves against those who do.

The United States is now undertaking a major strengthening of our defenses. It's an expensive effort, but we make it to protect the peace, knowing that a strong America is a safeguard for the independence and peace of others.

Both the United States and China are rich in human resources and human talent. What wonders lie before us if we practice the advice, Tong Li He Zuo—Connect strength, and work together?

Over the past 12 years, American and Chinese leaders have met frequently to discuss a host of issues. Often we have found agreement, but even when we have not, we've gained insight into each other, and we've learned to appreciate the other's perspectives on the world.

This process will continue, and it will flourish if we remember certain things. We must neither ignore our problems nor overstate them. We must never exaggerate our difficulties or send alarms for small reasons. We must remember that it is a delicate thing to oppose

the wishes of a friend, and when we're forced to do so, we must understand with each other.

I hope that when history looks back upon this new chapter in our relationship, these will be remembered as days when America and China accepted the challenge to strengthen the ties that bind us, to cooperate for greater prosperity among our people, and to strive for a more secure and just peace in the world.

You, the students at Fudan University, and the scholars at all the universities in China and America have a great role to play in both our countries' futures. From your ranks will come the understanding and skill the world will require in decades to come. Today's leaders can pave the way of the future. That is our responsibility. But it is always the younger generation who will make the future. It is you who will decide if a continuing, personal friendship can span the generations and the differences that divide us. In such friendship lies the hope of the world.

When he was a very young man, Zhou Enlai wrote a poem for a schoolmate who was leaving to study abroad. Zhou appreciated the responsibilities that separated them, but he also remembered fondly the qualities that made them friends. And his poem ends:

Promise, I pray, that someday

When task done, we go back farming,

We'll surely rent a plot of ground

And as pairing neighbors, let's live.

Well, let us, as pairing neighbors, live.

I've been happy to speak to you here, to meet you in this city that is so rich in significance for both our countries. Shanghai is a city of scholarship, a city of learning. Shanghai has been a window to the West. It is a city in which my country and yours issued the communique that began our modern friendship. It is the city where the Yangtze meets the East China Sea, which, itself, becomes the Pacific, which touches our shores.

My young friends, history is a river that may take us as it will. But we have the power to navigate, to choose direction, and make our passage together. The wind is up, the current is swift, and opportunity for a long and fruitful journey awaits us.

Generations hence will honor us for having begun the voyage, for moving on together and escaping the fate of the buried armies of Xi'an, the buried warriors who stood for centuries frozen in time, frozen in an unknowing enmity.

We have made our choice. Our new journey will continue. And may it always continue in peace and in friendship.

Thank you very much.

我们到达中国访问虽然仅有五天，所看到的名胜古迹却使我们终生难忘。这当中有从太空都能看到的巍峨壮观的万里长城，还有古城西安、秦始皇墓和出土的兵马俑。这些都是历史上的奇迹。

但是，我今天想和你们这所著名学府的年轻人谈谈未来，谈谈我们共同的未来，谈谈我们怎样才能发挥治学的才智和探索精神来了解彼此的情况，改变人类的生活。

首先，我代表我的国民对来听我演讲的诸位表示由衷的问候。

此外，我还带来一位你们的同胞的问候，也就是曾经在复旦就读的叶扬。他从复旦毕业，并在此担任英语教师。现在在美国哈佛大学攻读比较文学博士学位。

离开前，我的工作人员曾与他谈话。叶扬希望他的同胞知道他一切顺利。他正努力地写第二学期的论文，他非常想念你们。他请我向他的学生、同事、朋友和家人带个口信，他说："我想念大家。"能帮他这个忙，我非常高兴。

他想告诉你们，他期待回到复旦教学。谢校长，叶扬还想告诉您，他非常感谢您的鼓励，也珍惜您的友谊。他还说您是一位非常伟大的女性，也是一位很好的教师。听到他上学期拿了年级最优，相信您会感到非常自豪的。我们祝贺他的时候，他说："我自己没什么可自豪的，但是我为我的大学感到自豪。"

我想略微谈谈中美之间的教育交流计划。两国交换留学生，实际上并不是什么新事物，你们的谢校长曾在美国史密斯学院获得学位。史密斯学院也是我的夫人南希的母校。谢校长还在麻省理工学院学习过，这是美国最大的一所理工学院。

然而，最近几年以来，两国交换的留学生人数急剧增加。五年前中国去国外的留学生还只不过几百名，而现在中国在全世界的学者和学生已达两万多名，其中一半以上到美国学习。现在有一百多家美国大专院校和几乎同样多的中国大专院校建立了教育上的交流关系。

美国的"富布赖特奖学金计划"拨给中国的奖学金，比拨给任何其他国家的都多。在复旦任教的美国教授当中就有两位是"富布赖特教授"。还有二十位美国学生也在这里和大家一起学习，我们很为他们自豪。

美国学生在中国学习有广阔的天地。他们向中国学习如何监测和预报地震，学习中国在研究癌症的病因和治疗方面是如何取得这么多成就的。中国在神经外科、用草药治病等方面，有许多东西可供我们学习。我们也非常高兴有机会研究中国的语言、历史和现代社会。

你们也表示很愿意向我们学习，来美国学校学习电子和计算机科学、数学和工程学、物理学、管理学以及人文学科。在这些领域里，我们可以相互学习的地方很多。我们殷切希望从你们的探索精神中获益。两国之间相互学习是最近才有的事，很多这类活动只有五年的历史。但是我们彼此合作的领域还在不断增加。我们已经商定在贸易、技术、投资以及科学与管理专业知识的交流等方面进行更密切地合作。此外，我们刚刚还达成了一项重要的协议，通过和平利用核能来促进我们的技术和经济发展。

"核能的和平利用"条款是一个关键。我们的协议是建立在重要的防扩散原则基础之上的。不论是中国还是美国都不支持核扩散，也不会帮助任何其他国家得到或开发出任何核爆装置。

我们生活在一个动荡的世界中，美中两国都是伟大的国家，对减少战争危险都负有特别的责任。我们双方一致认为，为了使人类宝贵的文明能够在当代不毁于一旦，只有一种政策是合理的，那就是永远不打那种谁也打不赢的核战争。不管障碍看来有多大，我们永远不应放松削减战争武器的努力。我们丝毫也不能放松，直到把核武器从地球上彻底销毁。

只要我们奉行和平合作的方针，就有可能在将来取得巨大的进步。例如，我们期望与中国一起探讨是否有可能合作开发太空，这是符合世界人民的利益的。

我们的宇航员发现，在失重的宇宙环境中，将能够生产纯度更高、更加有效的药物，来治疗千百万人的心脏病和中风病。我们将能在轨道上试验制作"第八因子"，这是一种非常珍贵的稀有药物，可以治疗血友病。我们可以研究 β 细胞，用它来生产胰岛素，用它也许能够根治人类的糖尿病。

我们可以合作发射各种新型卫星，包括用于导航、气象预报、广播、电子计算机技术等方面的卫星。我们已经拥有化神奇为现实的技术。我们希望有一天，在复旦研究工程学问题的一个中国科学家，将能够同美国麻省理工学院一台计算机旁的科学家沟通联系，请他给予协助。同样，在美国波士顿的一位科学家，也将能够向上海的一位科学家寻求提供专业知识。而这种联系只需要几秒钟的时间就可以连接。

青年朋友们，这就是未来发展的方向。如果我们把才能和资源汇合起来，就能把太空这个尚未开拓的疆域变成一个新的和平疆域。

在自由交流知识方面，中国政府奉行加强对外联系的政策，这不仅活跃了中国的经济，而且为促进中美两国的共同利益开辟了新的渠道。你们已经打开了门户，我向你们保证，我们的门户也是敞开着的。

这些新发展同过去两国的关系相对照，令人感到特别兴奋。两国关系曾经疏远了许多年，两国为此付出了代价。十二年前情况开始变化，那是在我们共同努力之下促成的变化。在最近五年里，中国实行的对外开放政策，使我们开始比以往更加了解对方。

然而这一过程仅仅是个开端。时至今日，仍然有许多美国人觉得中国远在天涯海角，鲜为人知，令人心驰神往。

我们对中国确实心驰神往。各位可知道，中国已经在许多方面对美国的生活发生了影响。中国的影响，中国的成就，在美国到处可见。如果今天下午我是在华盛顿，只要望向窗外，便可以看到一男一女，身穿中国丝绸服装，在白宫门前的宾夕法尼亚大道上散步。他们可能正在前往国立人像馆去看中国艺术展览，看完展览以后，他们也许会漫步到国家美术馆，去看美籍华裔建筑师贝聿铭为该馆设计的新楼。然后他们可能会去一家中国餐馆吃晚饭，以此来结束一天的活动。

我们提到中国就会想起朝气，蓬勃向上的朝气。我们还想起并不总是与朝气并存的敏锐，洞察事物的敏锐和睿智头脑的敏锐。

赵总理在今年一月访问美国期间，看到了美国对待中国的态度。他在访问了几天以后说："从来没有料到，美国人民对中国人民怀着这样深厚的友情。"

我高兴地说，我也可以用同样的赞扬来回赠中国人民。我发现中国人民对美国人民怀有同样热烈和深厚的友情，这使我们感到非常高兴。

但是，在今天与大家见面和谈话以后，我感到我需要更多地了解中国人民。想来你们也有同感，也想更多地了解美国人民。

我想告诉你们一些关于我们的情况，也想同你们分享一些我自己的价值观念。

首先，美国占了半个美洲。我们常把美国称为"移民之国"，情况确实如此，美国人来自世界上的每一个角落。美国有世界上的每一个种族，每一种宗教，而且各种族、各宗教的人数不是少数，而是多数。纽约港的自由女神像说明了这一点。自由女神高擎着火炬欢迎所有来到我们国家成为我国公民的人。她已经迎来了数以百万的移民来到我们的国家，她还将继续下去。她，就是美国敞开

的大门。

所有来到我们国家的移民带来他们自己的音乐、文学、风俗和思想。最了不起、最令我们自豪的是他们不必放弃他们原有的一切来适应这片土地。事实上，正是他们所带来的一切才成就了美国。这种多样性不仅充实了美国，也塑造了美国。

新来的移民不断给美国带来新事物，这是一种传统，一直延续至今。今天，外国移民仍然不断前来美国，不断把他们的才智带到美国来，不断提高着美国人民的生活水平。下面让我介绍其中的几位，大家一定会知道他们的名字。

王安公司的电子计算机，现在已成为美国各地办公室里的必备之物。这些计算机是王安先生的天才和心血培育出来的，而王安先生本人是上海一所大学培养出来的。

贝聿铭先生设计的建筑，为美国的城市面貌增添了光彩。贝聿铭先生对建筑艺术的兴趣，是他在上海读书时就产生的。

荣获诺贝尔奖金的科学家李政道博士，丰富了我们对宇宙、对物质的基本特性的认识。他是在上海出生的。

我们赞赏这些人，尊敬这些人。你们为使他们成材做出了贡献，我们也要向你们致敬。

在美国，有时候我们会相互争执，美国是一个爱争论的民族，我们喜欢辩论。尽管我们彼此之间相互争执，但我们团结一致，组成一个整体。我们一起走过了两百多年，坚定不移的信念让我们团结在一起，我们默默地笃信忠贞不渝的信念。

我提请诸位注意我接下来要说的话，因为它对了解我的国家至关重要。我们信仰每一位男士、女士和孩子的尊严。我们的整个体制是建立在对每一个人的天分欣赏之上，是建立在每个人有做自己的决定，过自己的生活的特权之上。

我们深信"人人生而平等，他们享有造物者赋予的若干不可剥夺的权利——生命的权利、自由的权利和追求幸福的权利。"这就是我们的信念，每一个美国人都能背诵这句名言。散会以后，你们可以把这里的任何一位美国学生或教员拉到一旁，问问他能不能背诵这句出自美国建国文献《独立宣言》的名言。

我们通过国民的投票选举我们的政府，选择我们的国会和总统。我们称美国是"人民统治"，事实确实如此。

我来讲讲我们的国民品质。你们可能认为如此复杂的民族不可能有一种共同的品质，但是在许多基本方面我们是一致的。

我们是公正的人。我们从小受到的教育让我们不拿任何属于别人的一丝一毫。正如我前面所述，我们当中的大多数都是移民的孩子、孙子和曾孙，我们从前辈那里学到了要艰苦劳动。我们的民族靠着辛勤劳作白手起家，世界上再没有人比我们这些为自己奋斗的人更值得信任。而且，所有的人都在觊觎那些不属于自己的东西。

美国人民热爱自由，也愿意为维护别人的自由而战斗，而献身。四十年前，法西斯军队席卷欧洲大陆，美国人民挺身而出，投放战斗，为保卫受侵略的国家作出了重大牺牲。

法西斯军队席卷亚洲的时候，我们和你们并肩抗敌。在座的有些人会记得那时的情况，会记得美国的杜立德将军率领轰炸机队，飞越半个地球前来助战的事迹。有些飞行员在中国上空机毁人伤，你们还记得那些勇敢的小伙子吧？你们把它们藏起来，照料他们，给他们包扎伤口，你们救了他们很多人的命。

二战胜利之后，美国自动从曾经战斗的地区退出，没有留下永久的占领军。我们当时没有拿走别国的一寸土地，现在也不会。我

们记录在案的对他人自由和独立的崇尚是显而易见的。

美国人民是富有同情心的人民。当战争结束，美国人帮助重建同盟国，也包括我们的敌国。我们如此做，是希望帮助不良政府、不良政策下无辜的受害者们。因为只有他们繁荣昌盛，世界才会更加稳定。

美国人民是乐观的人民。像中国一样，美国继承了幅员辽阔的国土，有一望无际的崇山峻岭，沃土良田和无边草原。辽阔的国土使我们能用积极的眼光去看待一切事物，使我们充满希望。

美国人民热爱和平，厌恶战争。我们始终认为战争罪大恶极，是无谓的浪费。我们希望和我们的邻居、朋友和平相处，

美利坚民族还有另外一种特质，宗教信仰和信念对我们来说至关重要。我们的民族有诸多信仰，但是大多数美国人的信仰都源自《圣经》中的摩西，他让一个人从奴隶制中解脱出来；还有耶稣基督，他告诉我们要像爱自己一样爱自己的邻居，想让邻居怎样对待自己就要先那样对待邻居。

这一点也铸造了美利坚民族。我们期待别人好正是基于此。这也是为什么当听说有人不能靠自己的能力生存，时刻处在动荡之中时，我们感到悲痛的原因。

我们欢迎你们多多了解我们，人民之间的友谊就是这样开始的。而人民之间的友谊，是政府之间友谊的基础。

美中两国政府之间的沉默状态已告结束。过去的十二年里，两国人民重新相识。现在我们的关系日益成熟，正是为持久友谊奠定基础的时候。

我们大家都很清楚，有许多因素自然而然地使我们之间产生距离。例如时间和空间、不同的语言和价值观念、不同的文化和历史、

截然不同的政治制度。不承认这些差别是愚蠢的，为了友谊而掩盖真相也毫无意义，因为向壁虚构的友谊经受不住这个世界的严峻考验。

但是我们暂时可以把那些描写我们差别的字眼撇在一旁，想一想我们之间的共同点。我们是两个伟大的国家，分处在地球的两边。两国都是朝气蓬勃、力量强大的国家。你们是世界上人口最多的国家，我们是世界上技术最发达的国家。两国都在地球上自己的一边发挥着特殊的作用。

中美两国之间存在着一种均势平衡。你们当中的理科生可能会欣赏这个词。它代表了一种和谐、特殊的平衡。

早先有一些共同的政治关注将中美联系在一起，并在一些重大问题上双方达成一致。中美两国都反对非法残忍占领柬埔寨，共同谴责非法入侵阿富汗，共同出资保持朝鲜半岛的稳定，保证世界这一地区的和平。

中美两国都不是领土扩张主义者。我们对中国乃至世界各国的土地都没有扩张的欲望。我们也没有挑战你们的国界，没有引起你们的担忧。事实上，中美两国都尽力武装自己来抵御任何一个有扩张欲望的国家。

美国现在正承担着加大防御力量的重大责任。这是一项耗资的尝试，但是我们会以此来保证和平，要知道强大的美国是自身独立和他国安全的保证。

美中两国都拥有大量的人力资源和人才。只要我们通力合作，什么样的奇迹都能创造出来！

十二年来，美中两国领导曾就一系列问题举行过多次会谈。我们常常达成一致意见，即使不能达成一致意见，我们也能加深对彼此的认识，理解对方对世界事务的看法。

这种进程会继续下去，假使我们铭记历史，必将蓬勃发展。我们既不要忽视双方之间的问题，也不要夸大这些问题；既不要夸大困难，也无需小题大做。我们必须记得，回避朋友的好意是很微妙的事，当我们不得不这样做的时候，我们必须相互理解。

我希望当人们回顾历史上两国关系这一新篇章时，将不会忘记今天的情景。美国和中国为加强我们之间的纽带，为两国人民享有更高度的繁荣而合作，为争取世界更可靠和公正的和平，曾接受过时代的挑战。

复旦大学的学生，中国和美国所有大学的学者，肩负着两国未来的重任。今后几十年里，世界将需要你们这些人相互谅解，发挥才能。今天的领袖可以为未来铺平道路，这是我们的责任。但是未来终归要由年青的一代来创造。至于个人之间的持久友谊能不能弥合上下辈之间、国与国之间的分歧，就取决于你们了。世界的希望就寄托在这种友谊之上。

周恩来年轻的时候曾为一位准备出洋留学的同窗写过一首送别诗。他很钦佩他的同学争挑重任，负笈远行。他也十分珍惜他们之间的崇高友情。诗的结尾写道：

"险夷不变应尝胆，

道义争担敢息肩。

待得归农功满日，

它年预卜买邻钱。"

让我们像近邻一样生活在一起吧。

有机会在这里向大家讲话，在这个对两国都具有重要意义的城市同大家见面，我感到十分高兴。上海是一个学术之城，一个知识之城。上海历来是你们通向西方之窗，也是我们两国发表公报，始建新友谊的地方。长江是世界的大河之一，它波浪滚滚经上海流入东海，东海同太平洋汇合，太平洋的波涛汹涌，直达美国西海岸。

青年朋友们，历史是一条长河，它用波浪裹挟着我们。但是我们可以驾船航行，选择方向，同舟共济。风高潮急，一次富有成果的远行正在等待着我们。

我们的子孙后代会感谢我们开始的这段旅程，感谢我们推动了彼此的进步，避免了秦皇陵墓中被埋葬的军队那样的命运，那些矗立了几个世纪的将士凝固在时光里，凝结着无名的仇恨。

我们已经作出了选择。我们将继续我们新的旅程，但愿我们一路顺风，永远生活在友谊与和平之中。

谢谢你们！

第三节 精彩语录

We live in a troubled world, and the United States and China, as two great nations, share a special responsibility to help reduce the risks of war. We both agree that there can be only one sane policy to preserve our precious civilization in this modern age: A nuclear war cannot be won and must never be fought. And no matter how great the obstacles may seem, we must never stop our efforts to reduce the weapons of war. We must never stop at all until we see the day when nuclear arms have been banished from the face of this Earth.

我们生活在一个动荡的世界中，美中两国都是伟大的国家，对减少战争危险都负有特别的责任。我们双方一致认为，为了使人类宝贵的文明能够在当代不毁于一旦，只有一种政策是合理的，那就是永远不打那种谁也打不赢的核战争。不管障碍看来有多大，我们永远不应放松削减战争武器的努力。我们丝毫也不能放松，直到把核武器从地球上彻底销毁。

Your government's policy of forging closer ties in the free exchange of knowledge has not only enlivened your economy, it has opened the way to a new convergence of Chinese and American interests. You have opened the door, and let me assure you that ours is also open.

在自由交流知识方面，中国政府奉行加强对外联系的政策，这不仅活跃了中国的经济，而且为促进中美两国的共同利益开辟了新的渠道。你们已经打开了门户，我向你们保证，我们的门户也是敞开着的。

We associate China with vitality, enormous vitality, and something that does not always go along with that—subtlety, the subtlety of discerning and intelligent minds.

我们提到中国就会想起朝气，蓬勃向上的朝气。我们还想起并不总是与朝气并存的敏锐，洞察事物的敏锐和睿智头脑的敏锐。

We believe—and we believe it so deeply that Americans know these words by heart—we believe "that all men are created equal, that they are endowed by their Creator with certain unalienable Rights, that among those are Life, Liberty and the pursuit of Happiness."

我们深信这句名言："人人生而平等，他们享有造物者赋予的若干不可剥夺的权利——生命的权利、自由的权利和追求幸福的权利。"这就是我们的信念，每一个美国人都能背诵这句名言。

Now, you know, as I do, that there's much that naturally divides us: time and space, different languages and values, different cultures

and histories, and political systems that are fundamentally different. It would be foolish not to acknowledge these differences. There's no point in hiding the truth for the sake of a friendship, for a friendship based on fiction will not long withstand the rigors of this world.

我们大家都很清楚，有许多因素自然而然地使我们之间产生距离。例如时间和空间、不同的语言和价值观念、不同的文化和历史、截然不同的政治制度。不承认这些差别是愚蠢的，为了友谊而掩盖真相也毫无意义，因为向壁虚构的友谊经受不住这个世界的严峻考验。

My young friends, history is a river that may take us, as it will. But we have the power to navigate, to choose direction, and make our passage together. The wind is up, the current is swift, and opportunity for a long and fruitful journey awaits us.

青年朋友们，历史是一条长河，它用波浪裹挟着我们。但是我们可以驾船航行，选择方向，同舟共济。风高潮急，一次富有成果的远行正在等待着我们。

第四章

美国的精神觉醒

第一节 背景介绍

大国间的利益取舍往往能够决定一段时间内世界的局势发展。苏联从 20 世纪 70 年代中期加快了扩张的步伐，而苏联的发展使美国感到了极大的危机，美国认为苏联的扩张危及了他的根本利益。在这种情况下，苏美的矛盾和冲突加剧，两国关系逐步恶化。里根上台后对苏联奉行强硬方针。他大力扩充军备，想用不凡的实力求得和平。苏联则仍坚持扩张，继续致力于加强军事实力，紧逼美国，同美进行争夺。世界格局走上了两级分化。里根执政期间，苏美的矛盾和斗争较前几任总统时期更尖锐、复杂，它们的关系总的来说是紧张的。

如果说 20 世纪 70 年代前半期苏美关系比较缓和，1975 年欧安会的召开标志着缓和达到高潮，那么到 20 世纪 70 年代后半期，爆发了安哥拉事件，使这种缓和的关系逐渐转为激烈抗争，1979 年底阿富汗事件的爆发，则使缓和基本破裂。当时正在进行的限制战略武器谈判陷入困境，成为一张废纸。而美苏之间的各项裁军谈判也都陷入了僵局停滞不前。美苏之前展开了新的一轮大规模的军备竞赛。美国对苏入侵阿富汗采取了诸如抵制奥运会、粮食部分禁运、禁售尖端技术等一系列重大制裁措施，两国的外交关系降到最低水平。

20 世纪 70 年代初，美国侵越陷入困境，苏联乘美国实力急剧下降，迅速扩充实力，使苏美军事、经济力量对比发生有利于苏的变化，形成了苏攻美守的新态势。20 世纪 70 年代末 80 年代初随着苏联连续发动扩张攻势，两个超级大国的矛盾日益加深，争夺不断加剧，苏美之间出现了僵冷和紧张的必然结果。

在 20 世纪 80 年代中期之前，由于美国同苏联军力对比不利于美国的趋势难以根本改变，苏美争夺中苏攻美守态势仍将维持不变，而决心以实力遏制苏联的里根政府不会改变其强硬的对苏方针，这就决定了今后两国的抗争还要继续下去，它们之间的紧张关系也不会改变。里根上台后为改变军事上的颓势，采取空前规模的扩军方针，苏联为了争夺军事优势，决心采取相应措施对付。20 世纪 80 年代苏美两霸将不可避免地展开新一轮规模更大的军备竞赛，双方围绕这个问题上的争斗必将更加尖锐，这势必给它们的关系带来严重影响。两国关系中存在的限制战略武器谈判、欧洲战区核谈判、阿富汗、波兰等一系列重大问题，都是事关双方切身利益，对两国影响甚大的棘手问题，也是阻碍两国关系发展的重要因素。

前总统卡特为应付苏联的挑战，改变了对苏政策的指导思想，由过去强调缓和、裁军、合作转变为强调竞争、争夺和对抗。为了保护自己的切身利益，美国对苏战略作了重要调整。在军事上决定大幅度增加军费，力图扭转军力对比不利于美的发展趋势，改变在军事战略上的被动态势。同时改变了越战后对区域性冲突避免军事卷入的态度，针对苏联的南下战略，提出用武力保卫波斯湾地区的

卡特主义，并在印度洋作了一系列相应军事部署，防范苏联继续南进。美国从过去同苏搞缓和转为敦促盟国增加军备，协调抗苏。里根上台后把以实力遏制苏联扩张的政策定为本届政府的既定方针，对苏采取更加强硬的态度，苏美关系更趋紧张。一个要坚持谋求扩大势力范围，另一个决心遏制对方扩张地盘，这就必然导致双方利益发生尖锐的矛盾冲突。

进入 20 世纪 80 年代，苏美两国都认为，它们的关系降到了十多年来的最低点，进入了一个紧张阶段。里根就在这时走上了政坛。上台后他强调以实力求和平，把遏制苏联在全球扩张作为其对外政策的根本任务，对苏采取强硬政策。

里根采取了多种行动和措施大规模加强军事力量，增强实力地位。里根扩充军备的规模超过卡特。他提出了美国历史上最庞大的军事预算，1981 年度军费为 1,780 亿美元（比卡特多 68 亿），1982 年度高达 2,263 亿，并计划在今后五年里，军费总额将为 15,000 亿，每年实增 7%。

美国采取了较广泛的措施在全球范围加强战略部署，遏制苏联扩张。最突出的是加强美国在中东、海湾和印度洋的军事力量。如宣布在印度洋长期保持两个航母编队；在五年内用 150 亿美元建设快速部署部队；利用埃及、索马里等国提供的基地设施，加强美国在该地区的军事存在；通过军事和经济援助加强受到苏联扩张威胁的沙特、巴基斯坦等国的抗苏能力，派遣特使调停以叙冲突，力阻苏在中东扩大影响等。对阿富汗、波兰等问题，里根仍持强硬态度，声称苏联只有从阿撤军，才能指望根本上同美国改善关系，如对波兰入侵，必将对苏美关系产生严重后果。

同时里根重修同欧日盟国的关系，协调抗苏。里根执政后十分重视密切与盟国关系，协调对苏政策。里根利用频繁的外交来往和各种会议，同西欧盟国主要就增加军费、部署战区核武器、改进美欧战略分工、西班牙加入北约以及协调对波兰问题的对策等一系列重大问题进行磋商，作出一定的妥协和让步，使西欧国家坚持部署新型战区核武器，执行增加军费的计划，同意为在波斯湾抗苏出力，并在波兰问题上采取同美一致的政策，基本顶住了苏联的新和平攻势。对日本，里根政府则继续促其增加军费，加强防务，在亚太地区承担更多义务。

虽然里根做了诸多的措施遏制苏联，但他既受国力不足的限制，又受国内外多种因素的制约。这就决定了其对苏政策与其前任一样不可避免地具有妥协的一面。由于国内和欧洲盟国的压力，里根取消了对苏粮食禁运，同意同苏举行欧洲战区核谈判，并表示不排除到一定阶段同苏进行其他问题的会谈，反映了他对苏的强硬政策是有一定限度的。

里根在宣布生产中子弹后即写信给勃列日涅夫，建议在今后某个时候举行首脑会晤，还表示美国愿同苏建立比较广泛的互利关系。这些都表明里根政府对苏政策的两重性。当然里根对苏政策的妥协和摆动与卡特时期有所不同，虽然在某个时候和某些方面他可能作出妥协，但从总的方面看，强硬是其对苏政策的主导方面。

两国总的关系在保持紧张状态的前提下，有可能出现局部妥协。由于美国国力衰弱，国内既面临严重的经济衰退，又有诸多方面的掣肘，与盟国特别是西欧在利益和政策上存在各种分歧，使它在对苏推行强硬方针时受到内外各种因素的牵制和影响。而苏联则由于经济增长率不断下降，经济拮据，实力不足，对美国与其进行巨大规模的军备竞赛使其经济受到严重影响深感不安。其侵阿后一直未能摆脱孤立

困境，由于波兰问题又面临东欧后院的动荡，古巴、越南、阿富汗的包袱沉重，内外困难重重，使它推行扩张政策也受到很大的制约。

因此，两国在进行激烈抗争的同时，出于各自的内外困难和需要，都在谋求必要的妥协。如有些谈判明知难于达成协议，但为了追求表面价值，也可能陆续开谈，甚至实现最高级会晤。美国迫于内外压力，主动对苏联降调，强硬的态度有所缓和，并决定在之后三年中将军事开支削减130亿美元。苏联虽然表面气壮如牛，在宣传上对美国严厉攻击，摆出不妥协的样子，而实际上生怕"缓和"被葬送。在一些重大问题上，如波兰问题上不得不克制行事。这都说明美苏在激烈争夺中都不想搞到剑拔弩张的地步，都有妥协的需要。但是苏美的基本矛盾难以克服，它们的根本利益冲突无法调和，它们之间的谈判也只能是旷日持久的聋子对话。因此它们的妥协也只能是有限的、表面的，苏美两国要恢复到20世纪70年代前期的缓和时代是再无可能了。

第二节 里根在美国全国福音派联会年会上的演讲

Thank you. Thank you very much.

And, Reverend Clergy all, Senator Hawkins, distinguished members of the Florida congressional delegation, and all of you: I can't tell you how you have warmed my heart with your welcome. I'm delighted to be here today.

Those of you in the National Association of Evangelicals are known for your spiritual and humanitarian work. And I would be especially remiss if I didn't discharge right now one personal debt of gratitude. Thank you for your prayers. Nancy and I have felt their presence many times in many ways. And believe me, for us they've made all the difference.

The other day in the East Room of the White House at a meeting there, someone asked me whether I was aware of all the people out there who were praying for the President. And I had to say, "Yes, I am. I've felt it. I believe in intercessionary prayer." But I couldn't help

but say to that questioner after he'd asked the question that—or at least say to them that if sometimes when he was praying he got a busy signal, it was just me in there ahead of him. I think I understand how Abraham Lincoln felt when he said, "I have been driven many times to my knees by the overwhelming conviction that I had nowhere else to go." From the joy and the good feeling of this conference, I go to a political reception. Now, I do not know why, but that bit of scheduling reminds me of a story which I will share with you.

An evangelical minister and a politician arrived at Heaven's gate one day together. And St. Peter, after doing all the necessary formalities, took them in hand to show them where their quarters would be. And he took them to a small, single room with a bed, a chair, and a table and said this was for the clergyman. And the politician was a little worried about what might be in store for him. And he couldn't believe it then when St. Peter stopped in front of a beautiful mansion with lovely grounds, many servants, and told him that these would be his quarters.

And he couldn't help but ask, he said, "But wait, how—there's something wrong—how do I get this mansion while that good and holy man only gets a single room?" And St. Peter said, "You have to understand how things are up here. We've got thousands and thousands of clergy. You're the first politician who ever made it."

But I don't want to contribute to a stereotype. So I tell you there are a great many God-fearing, dedicated, noble men and women in public life, present company included. And yes, we need your help to keep us ever-mindful of the ideas and the principles that brought us into the public arena in the first place. The basis of those ideals and principles is a commitment to freedom and personal liberty that, itself is grounded in the much deeper realization that freedom prospers only where the blessings of God are avidly sought and humbly accepted.

The American experiment in democracy rests on this insight. Its discovery was the great triumph of our Founding Fathers, voiced by William Penn when he said: "If we will not be governed by God, we must be governed by tyrants." Explaining the inalienable rights of men, Jefferson said, "The God who gave us life, gave us liberty at the same time." And it was George Washington who said "of all the dispositions and habits which lead to political prosperity, religion and morality are indispensable supports."

And finally, that shrewdest of all observers of American democracy, Alexis de Tocqueville, put it eloquently after he had gone on a search for the secret of America's greatness and genius—and he said: "Not until I went into the churches of America and heard her pulpits aflame with righteousness did I understand the greatness and the genius of America. America is good. And if America ever ceases to be good, America will cease to be great."

Well, I'm pleased to be here today with you who are keeping America great by keeping her good. Only through your work, prayers, and those of millions of others can we hope to survive this perilous century and keep alive this experiment in liberty, this last, best hope of man.

I want you to know that this administration is motivated by a political philosophy that sees the greatness of America in you, her people, and in your families, churches, neighborhoods, communities: the institutions that foster and nourish values like concern for others

and respect for the rule of law under God.

Now, I don't have to tell you that this puts us in opposition to, or at least out of step with, a—a prevailing attitude of many who have turned to a modern-day secularism, discarding the tried and time-tested values upon which our very civilization is based. No matter how well intentioned, their value system is radically different from that of most Americans. And while they proclaim that they're freeing us from superstitions of the past, they've taken upon themselves the job of superintending us by government rule and regulation. Sometimes their voices are louder than ours, but they are not yet a majority.

An example of that vocal superiority is evident in a controversy now going on in Washington. And since I'm involved, I've been waiting to hear from the parents of young America. How far are they willing to go in giving to government their prerogatives as parents?

Let me state the case as briefly and simply as I can. An organization of citizens, sincerely motivated, deeply concerned about the increase in illegitimate births and abortions involving girls well below the age of consent, some time ago established a nationwide network of clinics to offer help to these girls and, hopefully, alleviate this situation. Now, again, let me say, I do not fault their intent. However, in their well-intentioned effort, these clinics decided to provide advice and birth control drugs and devices to underage girls without the knowledge of their parents.

For some years now, the federal government has helped with funds to subsidize these clinics. In providing for this, the Congress decreed that every effort would be made to maximize parental participation. Nevertheless, the drugs and devices are prescribed without getting parental consent or giving notification after they've done so. Girls termed "sexually active" —and that has replaced the word "promiscuous" —are given this help in order to prevent illegitimate birth or abortion.

Well, we have ordered clinics receiving federal funds to notify the parents such help has been given. One of the nation's leading newspapers has created the term "squeal rule" in editorializing against us for doing this, and we're being criticized for violating the privacy of young people. A judge has recently granted an injunction against an enforcement of our rule. I have watched TV panel shows discuss this issue, seen columnists pontificating on our error, but no one seems to mention morality as playing a part in the subject of sex.

Is all of Judeo–Christian tradition wrong? Are we to believe that something so sacred can be looked upon as a purely physical thing with no potential for emotional and psychological harm? And isn't it the parents' right to give counsel and advice to keep their children from making mistakes that may affect their entire lives?

Many of us in government would like to know what parents think about this intrusion in their family by government. We're going to fight in the courts. The right of parents and the rights of family take precedence over those of Washington–based bureaucrats and social engineers.

But the fight against parental notification is really only one example of many attempts to water down traditional values and even abrogate the original terms of American democracy. Freedom prospers when religion is vibrant and the rule of law under God is acknowledged. When our Founding Fathers passed the First

Amendment, they sought to protect churches from government interference. They never intended to construct a wall of hostility between government and the concept of religious belief itself.

The evidence of this permeates our history and our government. The Declaration of Independence mentions the Supreme Being no less than four times. "In God We Trust" is engraved on our coinage. The Supreme Court opens its proceedings with a religious invocation. And the members of Congress open their sessions with a prayer. I just happen to believe the schoolchildren of the United States are entitled to the same privileges as Supreme Court justices and congressmen.

Last year, I sent the Congress a constitutional amendment to restore prayer to public schools. Already this session, there is growing bipartisan support for the amendment, and I am calling on the Congress to act speedily to pass it and to let our children pray.

Perhaps some of you read recently about the Lubbock school case, where a judge actually ruled that it was unconstitutional for a school district to give equal treatment to religious and nonreligious student groups, even when the group meetings were being held during the students' own time. The First Amendment never intended to require government to discriminate against religious speech.

Senators Denton and Hatfield have proposed legislation in the Congress on the whole question of prohibiting discrimination against religious forms of student speech. Such legislation could go far to restore freedom of religious speech for public school students. And I hope the Congress considers these bills quickly. And with your help, I think it's possible we could also get the constitutional amendment through the Congress this year.

More than a decade ago, a Supreme Court decision literally wiped off the books of fifty states statutes protecting the rights of unborn children. Abortion on demand now takes the lives of up to one and a half million unborn children a year. Human life legislation ending this tragedy will someday pass the Congress, and you and I must never rest until it does. Unless and until it can be proven that the unborn child is not a living entity, then its right to life, liberty, and the pursuit of happiness must be protected.

You may remember that when abortion on demand began, many, and indeed, I am sure many of you, warned that the practice would lead to a decline in respect for human life, that the philosophical premises used to justify abortion on demand would ultimately be used to justify other attacks on the sacredness of human life—infanticide or mercy killing. Tragically enough, those warnings proved all too true. Only last year a court permitted the death by starvation of a handicapped infant.

I have directed the Health and Human Services Department to make clear to every health care facility in the United States that the Rehabilitation Act of 1973 protects all handicapped persons against discrimination based on handicaps, including infants. And we have taken the further step of requiring that each and every recipient of federal funds who provides health care services to infants must post and keep posted in a conspicuous place a notice stating "discriminatory failure to feed and care for handicapped infants in this facility is prohibited by federal law." It also lists a twenty-four-hour; toll-free number so that nurses and others may report violations in time to save the infant's life.

In addition, recent legislation introduced by—in the Congress by Representative Henry Hyde of Illinois not only increases restrictions on publicly financed abortions, it also addresses this whole problem of infanticide. I urge the Congress to begin hearings and to adopt legislation that will protect the right of life to all children, including the disabled or handicapped.

Now, I'm sure that you must get discouraged at times, but there you've done better than you know, perhaps. There's a great spiritual awakening in America, a renewal of the traditional values that have been the bedrock of America's goodness and greatness.

One recent survey by a Washington-based research council concluded that Americans were far more religious than the people of other nations were; 95 percent of those surveyed expressed a belief in God and a huge majority believed the Ten Commandments had real meaning in their lives. And another study has found that an overwhelming majority of Americans disapprove of adultery, teenage sex, pornography, abortion, and hard drugs. And this same study showed a deep reverence for the importance of family ties and religious belief.

I think the items that we've discussed here today must be a key part of the nation's political agenda. For the first time the Congress is openly and seriously debating and dealing with the prayer and abortion issues and that's enormous progress right there. I repeat: America is in the midst of a spiritual awakening and a moral renewal. And with your biblical keynote, I say today, "Yes, let justice roll on like a river, righteousness like a never-failing stream."

Now, obviously, much of this new political and social consensus

I've talked about is based on a positive view of American history, one that takes pride in our country's accomplishments and record. But we must never forget that no government schemes are going to perfect man.

We know that living in this world means dealing with what philosophers would call the phenomenology of evil or, as theologians would put it, the doctrine of sin.There is sin and evil in the world, and we're enjoined by Scripture and the Lord Jesus to oppose it with all our might. Our nation, too, has a legacy of evil with which it must deal. The glory of this land has been its capacity for transcending the moral evils of our past. For example, the long struggle of minority citizens for equal rights, once a source of disunity and civil war is now a point of pride for all Americans. We must never go back. There is no room for racism, anti-Semitism, or other forms of ethnic and racial hatred in this country.

I know that you've been horrified, as have I, by the resurgence of some hate groups preaching bigotry and prejudice. Use the mighty voice of your pulpits and the powerful standing of your churches to denounce and isolate these hate groups in our midst. The commandment given us is clear and simple: "Thou shall love thy neighbor as thyself."

But whatever sad episodes exist in our past, any objective observer must hold a positive view of American history, a history that has been the story of hopes fulfilled and dreams made into reality. Especially in this century, America has kept alight the torch of freedom, but not just for ourselves but for millions of others around the world.

And this brings me to my final point today. During my first press conference as president, in answer to a direct question, I pointed out that, as good Marxist–Leninists, the Soviet leaders have openly and publicly declared that the only morality they recognize is that which will further their cause, which is world revolution. I think I should point out I was only quoting Lenin, their guiding spirit, who said in 1920 that they repudiate all morality that proceeds from supernatural ideas—that's their name for religion—or ideas that are outside class conceptions. Morality is entirely subordinate to the interests of class war. And everything is moral that is necessary for the annihilation of the old, exploiting social order and for uniting the proletariat.

Well, I think the refusal of many influential people to accept this elementary fact of Soviet doctrine illustrates a historical reluctance to see totalitarian powers for what they are. We saw this phenomenon in the 1930s. We see it too often today.

This doesn't mean we should isolate ourselves and refuse to seek an understanding with them. I intend to do everything I can to persuade them of our peaceful intent, to remind them that it was the West that refused to use its nuclear monopoly in the forties and fifties for territorial gain and which now proposes 50 percent cut in strategic ballistic missiles and the elimination of an entire class of land–based, intermediate–range nuclear missiles.

At the same time, however, they must be made to understand we will never compromise our principles and standards. We will never give away our freedom. We will never abandon our belief in God. And we will never stop searching for a genuine peace. But we can assure none of these things America stands for through the so–called nuclear freeze solutions proposed by some.

The truth is that a freeze now would be a very dangerous fraud, for that is merely the illusion of peace. The reality is that we must find peace through strength.

I would agree to a freeze if only we could freeze the Soviets' global desires. A freeze at current levels of weapons would remove any incentive for the Soviets to negotiate seriously in Geneva and virtually end our chances to achieve the major arms reductions, which we have proposed. Instead, they would achieve their objectives through the freeze.

A freeze would reward the Soviet Union for its enormous and unparalleled military buildup. It would prevent the essential and long overdue modernization of United States and allied defenses and would leave our aging forces increasingly vulnerable. And an honest freeze would require extensive prior negotiations on the systems and numbers to be limited and on the measures to ensure effective verification and compliance. And the kind of a freeze that has been suggested would be virtually impossible to verify. Such a major effort would divert us completely from our current negotiations on achieving substantial reductions.

A number of years ago, I heard a young father, a very prominent young man in the entertainment world, addressing a tremendous gathering in California. It was during the time of the cold war, and communism and our own way of life were very much on people's minds. And he was speaking to that subject. And suddenly, though, I heard him saying, "I love my little girls more than anything." And I said to myself, "Oh, no, don't. You can't—don't say that." But I had

underestimated him. He went on: "I would rather see my little girls die now; still believing in God, than have them grow up under communism and one day die no longer believing in God."

There were thousands of young people in that audience. They came to their feet with shouts of joy. They had instantly recognized the profound truth in what he had said, with regard to the physical and the soul and what was truly important.

Yes, let us pray for the salvation of all of those who live in that totalitarian darkness. Pray they will discover the joy of knowing God. But until they do, let us be aware that while they preach the supremacy of the State, declare its omnipotence over individual man, and predict its eventual domination of all peoples on the earth, they are the focus of evil in the modern world.

It was C.S. Lewis who, in his unforgettable *Screw Tape Letters*, wrote: "The greatest evil is not done now in those sordid 'dens of crime' that Dickens loved to paint. It is not even done in concentration camps and labor camps. In those, we see its result. But it is conceived and ordered; moved, seconded, carried and minuted in clear, carpeted, warmed, and well-lighted offices, by quiet men with white collars and cut fingernails and smooth-shaven cheeks who do not need to raise their voice."

Well, because these quiet men do not raise their voices, because they sometimes speak in soothing tones of brotherhood and peace, because, like other dictators before them, they are always making "their final territorial demand," some would have us accept them at their word and accommodate ourselves to their aggressive impulses. But if history teaches anything, it teaches that simpleminded appeasement or wishful thinking about our adversaries is folly. It means the betrayal of our past, the squandering of our freedom.

So, I urge you to speak out against those who would place the United States in a position of military and moral inferiority. You know, I've always believed that old Screw Tape reserved his best efforts for those of you in the Church. So, in your discussions of the nuclear freeze proposals, I urge you to beware the temptation of pride—the temptation of blithely declaring yourselves above it all and label both sides equally at fault, to ignore the facts of history and the aggressive impulses of an evil empire, to simply call the arms race a giant misunderstanding and thereby remove yourself from the struggle between right and wrong and good and evil.

I ask you to resist the attempts of those who would have you withhold your support for our efforts, this administration's efforts, to keep America strong and free, while we negotiate real and verifiable reductions in the world's nuclear arsenals and one day, with God's help, their total elimination.

While America's military strength is important, let me add here that I've always maintained that the struggle now going on for the world will never be decided by bombs or rockets, by armies or military might. The real crisis we face today is a spiritual one; at root, it is a test of moral will and faith.

Whittaker Chambers, the man whose own religious conversion made him a witness to one of the terrible traumas of our time, the Hiss–Chambers case, wrote that the crisis of the Western world exists to the degree in which the West is indifferent to God, the degree to which it collaborates in communism's attempt to make man stand

alone without God. Then he said, for Marxism-Leninism is actually the second-oldest faith, first proclaimed in the Garden of Eden with the words of temptation, "Ye shall be as gods."

The Western world can answer this challenge, he wrote, "But only provided that its faith in God and the freedom He enjoins is as great as communism's faith in man."

I believe we shall rise to the challenge. I believe that communism is another sad, bizarre chapter in human history whose last—last pages even now are being written. I believe this because the source of our strength in the quest for human freedom is not material, but spiritual. And because it knows no limitation, it must terrify and ultimately triumph over those who would enslave their fellow man. For in the words of Isaiah: "He giveth power to the faint; and to them that have no might He increased strength. But they that wait upon the Lord shall renew their strength; they shall mount up with wings as eagles; they shall run, and not be weary."

Yes, change your world. One of our Founding Fathers, Thomas Paine, said, "We have it within our power to begin the world over again." We can do it, doing together what no one church could do by itoolf.

God bless you and thank you very much.

谢谢大家！非常感谢。

尊敬的宗教领袖们、霍金斯参议员、尊贵的弗罗里达国会代表团的成员、先生们：你们的欢迎让我感受到无法言表的温暖。今天在这里我感到非常愉快。

全国福音派联会的人士们所拥有的人道主义精神名闻遐迩。如果我不先向你们表达我的感激之情,我就太过傲慢无礼了。感谢你们的祈祷。南希和我经常能感受到你们就在身边的温暖。相信我,对我们来说,你们非常重要。

有一天,在白宫的东厅举行会议时,有人问我,是否注意到那些在外面一直为总统祈祷的人群。我说:"是的,我注意到了。我能感受到这一点。我相信代祷的作用。"但我又情不自禁地要告诉他——实际上也是对在场的所有人说,"如果有时候他在祈祷时得不到响应,那是因为我当时已经在上帝面前了。"亚伯拉罕·林肯说:"当我深信自己走投无路时,我总是要向上帝跪下呼求。"我想我理解林肯说这话时的感受。怀着对这次聚会的愉快心情和美好感受,我要转入政治话题。我不知道为什么,但那个日程安排让我想起一个故事。

有一天,一位福音派牧师和一个政客来到天堂的大门前。圣彼得办完了所有必要的手续后,领着他们来到各自的住处。他先领着他们来到一个小单间,里面只有一张床、一把椅子和一张桌子,说这是为牧师准备的。看到这个情形,政客有点惴惴不安,不知道等待他的将会是什么。

当圣彼得领着他来到一所富丽堂皇、仆佣成群的大宅子时,他简直不相信自己的眼睛。他禁不住问彼得:"等等,有没有搞错?我怎么会有这样的寓所,而那个虔诚圣洁的人只得到一个单间?"彼得回答道:"你要明白,这里是物以稀为贵。我们已经有了数不清的牧师,而你是来这里的第一位政客。"

我说这个故事并不是要为这些陈词滥调助兴。而是要告诉你们,包括本人所在的部门,许许多多担任公职的人都是敬畏上帝、甘于

奉献、品格高贵的人。我们需要你们的帮助，以使我们得以铭记那些将我们第一次带入政治舞台的理念与原则。这些理念与原则的基础是对自由和个人权利的信守，而这种信守本身又是建立在深刻的体察上。即只有在热切探求和谦卑地领受上帝祝福的地方，自由才会繁荣兴旺。

美国人对于民主的试验是基于对上帝虔诚基础之上的。它的发现是国父们的伟大胜利，威廉·佩恩说："如果我们不愿受治于上帝，我们必受治于暴君。"在诠释不可剥夺的人权时，杰弗逊说："上天在赐予我们生命的同时也赐予了我们自由。"华盛顿说："在导致政治昌盛的各种意向和习惯中，宗教和道德是必不可少的支柱。"

最后，当探究美国何以如此伟大和富有创造力的秘密时，托克维尔这位对于美国民主最为敏锐的观察家雄辩地指出："当我走进美国的教堂，听到闪耀着公义之火的布道时，我才真正明白美国何以如此伟大和天赋非凡。美国人是虔信上帝的。而一旦美国不再虔诚，也将不再伟大。"

今天能与你们这些通过保持美国人的虔诚而使美国继续伟大的人士相聚，我感到非常愉快。只有通过你们和其他成千上万人的工作和祈祷，才能使我们在这个危机四伏的世纪有望幸存下来，并使自由这一人类最美好的希望生机勃勃。

我希望你们知道，我们的行政部门是由一种政治哲学推动的，这一政治哲学在你们、你们的家庭、教会、邻里和社区中间发现了美国的伟大：即各种制度均致力于鼓励和培植诸如关心他人和尊重上帝之下法治之类的价值观。

现在，你们想必与我一样清楚，正是这些价值观使我们与流行于当下许多人中间的态度大相径庭，或与他们格格不入。他们奉行一种现代化的世俗主义，将我们的文明赖以立基的价值观视如粪土，尽管这些价值观坚实可靠并经过时间的检验。不管他们出于何种善意，他们的价值体系与大多数美国人所持的立场截然不同。虽然他们宣称，他们正使我们从对过去的迷信中解放出来，但他们从事的工作却是借助政府的统治和威权来监控我们。有时候他们的嗓门似乎比我们大，但他们从未赢得多数。

那种调门拔高的例子，在最近华盛顿的一场争论中显而易见。自从我卷入这场争论以来，我就期待着能听到美国年轻人父母们的想法。他们究竟愿意向政府移交多少他们作为人之父母的特权？

让我尽可能简明扼要地说一下这个事例。一个动机纯正、对于日益增加的少年非法生育和堕胎现象深感关切的公民团体，不久前成立了一个全国性的医疗诊所网络，向那些不到法定年龄的女孩子们提供帮助，并希望能减轻她们所面临的困境。我要说，我并不对他们的意图吹毛求疵。然而，在这项意愿良好的努力中，这些诊所居然决定在未征求她们父母意见的情况下，向这些女孩子提供节育建议、药物和方法。

几年来，联邦政府一直向这些诊所提供资助。在提供资助时，国会要求采取一切措施以使父母的参与最大化。然而，医生在开药或教授方法时，事先并没有征得父母的同意，事后也没有向他们说明。他们就是这样帮助那些被称为"性活跃"而不是"乱交"的女孩子们防止非法生育或堕胎的。

是的，我们已经责令那些接受联邦拨款的诊所必须要向父母们通报他们所提供的帮助。而一份全国性的大报却在编者按中杜撰了一个"告密规则"来对我们进行指控，批评我们侵犯了年轻人的"隐私权"。一位法官最近发布了一项禁令，阻止我们实施这项措施。我看

过有关这个话题的电视讨论，专栏作家们在里面一本正经地谴责我们的"错误"，但似乎没人提及在性问题上的道德成分。

难道犹太基督教传统全都错了吗？难道我们必须相信那些如此神圣的东西只与肉体相关而不会造成感情和心理上的伤害吗？父母们难道没有权利向他们的子女提出忠告和建议，以避免他们犯下有可能贻恨终生的大错吗？

我们政府中的许多人都想知道父母们在家里是如何思考这一由政府造成的局面的。我们会在法庭抗争下去。父母的权利以及家庭的权利优先于那些以华盛顿为基地的官僚们和社会工程师们的权利。

但是，反对告知父母仅是企图淡化传统价值观，甚至废除美国民主根本原则的众多事例中的一例而已。自由的繁荣有赖于宗教的兴旺以及人们对上帝之下法治的尊重。当国父们通过第一修正案时，他们是在谋求使教会免于政府的干预。他们从未打算在政府和宗教信仰之间树起一道敌视之墙。

我们的历史和政府中处处都有关于此一事实的证据。独立宣言中提到上帝的次数不少于四次。"我们信仰上帝"这句话就镌刻在我们的钱币上。最高法院以宗教祈祷来启动它的司法程序，国会议员们以祈祷来揭开会议的序幕，而我也碰巧相信美国的学童们享有与最高法院大法官和国会议员们同样的特权。

去年，我向国会递交了一个宪法修正案，要求恢复公立学校的祈祷活动。而在这届国会开会期间，两党中有越来越多的人支持这项修正案，我呼吁国会尽快通过该案，以使我们的孩子们能够祈祷。

也许你们中的一些人看过最近发生的卢伯克学校案，在此案中，一个法官宣布，学校给予有宗教信仰的学生和无宗教信仰的学生同等待遇其实是不合宪的，即使聚会是在学生课余时间进行也是如此。

第一修正案从未打算要求政府歧视宗教演讲。

丹顿和哈特菲尔德参议员已经在国会提交了一项法案，禁止对宗教性的学生演讲形式予以歧视。这项立法将足以恢复公立学校学生在宗教方面的言论自由。我希望国会能够迅速地考虑这些议案。靠着你们的帮助，我想我们很有可能在今年就获得这一宪法修正案。

十年前，最高法院的一项决定逐一抹去了五十个州关于保护胎儿权利的法规条款。有求必应式的堕胎每年至少要夺去 150 万胎儿的生命。终结这一悲剧的人类生命法案迟早有一天要在国会通过，不达目的我们决不罢休。除非有证据证明胎儿不是一个生命体，否则它的生命权、它的自由和它追求幸福的权利就必须得到保护。

你们可能还记得，当有求必应的堕胎刚开始时，许多人（这其中也包括你们中的许多人）都警告说，这一措施会使人们不再尊重生命，而被用于使堕胎合法化的哲学前提最终也会被用来为诸如杀婴或安乐死等其他蔑视生命神圣的行为做辩护。不幸的是，这些警告一一验证了。去年就有一家法院允许饿死一名残疾儿童。

我已经指示卫生及公共事务部向每一家美国卫生保健机构讲清楚，1973 年通过的康复法案保护所有的残疾人，反对任何基于残疾而产生的歧视，包括儿童。我们还采取了进一步的措施，要求每一个接受联邦拨款的婴幼儿保健机构必须在显眼位置始终张贴布告："基于歧视原因未对残疾婴幼儿进行喂食和照顾的行为均为联邦法律所禁止。"机构还必须列出一个二十四小时的免费电话号码，使护士及其他人能及时报告侵害事件，以拯救婴儿的生命。

另外，最近由伊利诺斯州的众议员亨利·海德提交的立法，不仅增加了对堕胎公款报销的限制，而且还关注杀婴问题。我敦促国会举行听证会并通过该法案，以保护所有孩子们的生命权，包括那

些残疾儿童的生命权。

现在，我肯定你们有时会感到灰心丧气，但也许你们所做的比你们所知的还要好。美国正经历一次精神上的觉醒，那为美国的虔诚和伟大奠基的传统价值观正在复兴。

一个设在华盛顿的研究理事会最近做了一个调查，得出的结果是美国人要比其他国家的人民虔诚得多。95％的被调查者表示信仰上帝，绝大多数人相信十诫在他们的生活中具有现实意义。另一个研究发现，压倒性多数的美国人不赞成通奸、少年性交、色情描写、堕胎和毒品。这些如出一辙的研究表明，人们深切尊重家庭纽带和宗教信仰的重要性。

我想我们今天讨论的课题一定会在国家的政治日程中发挥关键作用。这是国会首次就祈祷和堕胎问题进行公开而认真的辩论，这本身就是一项巨大的进步。我重申美国正处在精神觉醒和道德复兴之中。今天我要用《圣经》中的话说："唯愿公平如江河滔滔，使公义如溪水潺潺。"

很明显我所谈及的这种崭新的政治和社会共识中的大部分，立基于对美国历史的正面评价上，它以我们国家的历史成就为荣。但我们必须永远不要忘记，没有哪个政府计划会导致人的完美。

我们知道生活在这世界上就意味着要与哲学家所谓的邪恶或神学家所称的罪恶做斗争。世界上存在着罪恶与邪恶，而圣经和主耶稣呼召我们用一己之力去与之抗争。我们国家同样也拥有一份必须予以抵制的邪恶流毒。这片土地的荣耀之处就在于它有能力超越我们曾有过的道德罪恶。例如，少数族裔的公民为着争取平等权利而展开的长期抗争一度引发了分裂与内战，而现在却成为全体美国人为之自豪的一个亮点。我们决不会回到过去。在这个国家我们不会容忍种族主义、反犹太主义或其他各种形式的民族及种族仇恨。

我知道你们一直和我一样，对于一些散布固执偏见的讨厌团伙的复活而忧心忡忡。请用你们洪亮的布道和坚定的立场抨击我们中间这些令人憎恶的团伙。上帝赐予我们的诫命清晰而直率："要爱邻人如己。"

无论我们曾经有过什么样的不幸插曲，任何客观的观察家都会对美国的历史持积极的看法。我们的历史就是希望得以实现，梦想得以成真的动人故事。特别是在本世纪，美国使自由的火炬经久不息，不仅是为了我们自己，还为了全世界成千上万的人民。

由此我将谈及今天的最后一个话题。在我作为总统举行的第一次记者招待会上，在回答一个直率的问题时，我曾指出，苏联领导人是不错的马列主义者，他们开诚布公地宣称，他们所承认的唯一道德就是推动他们的事业，就是世界革命。我想我应该指出，这里我只引用了他们的精神导师列宁的话，他在 1920 年曾说，他们摒弃一切源于超自然观念的道德——那是他们给宗教下的定义——或与阶级学说无关的观念。道德完全服务于阶级斗争的需要。一种东西是否道德，取决于它是否为消灭旧的、剥削性的社会秩序和统一无产阶级的事业所必需。

我想许多有影响的人士拒绝接受苏联教条的这一基本观点，体现了对于极权主义本质的历史性抗拒。我们在 20 世纪 30 年代就目睹了这种抗拒。今天我们依然到处可见这种抗拒。

但这不意味着我们应该自我孤立并且拒绝寻求与他们的谅解。我打算尽一切努力去使他们相信我们的和平意愿，我要提醒他们，是西方在 20 世纪 40 年代和 50 年代拒绝利用其在核技术方面的垄断地位以扩张领土，同样是西方在今天提议削减 50％的战略弹道导弹，

以及销毁全部的陆基中程核导弹。

但是同时，他们也必须明白，我们永远不会拿我们的原则和准则讨价还价。我们永远不会出让我们的自由。我们永远不会背弃对上帝的信仰。我们也永远不会停止谋求一种真正的和平。但我们不能保证美国所支持的这些东西能够通过某些人士提出的所谓核冻结方案得到维护。

真实情况却是，现在的冻结将会成为一种非常危险的欺诈，因为它仅仅是和平的幻象。实际上我们必须通过实力来寻求和平。

只有当我们能够冻结苏联的全球野心时，我才会同意某种冻结。在当前水准下的武器冻结将使苏联在日内瓦与我们进行认真谈判的动机不复存在，事实上它会断送我们提出的削减主要军备的机会，更有甚者他们会通过冻结来达成他们的目的。

一次冻结给予苏联的奖赏就是庞大而且无与伦比的军事积累。而美国及盟国的国防现代化却会受到阻止，从而使我们日趋老化的军事力量弱不禁风。一种诚实的冻结会就限制的系统和数量、确保有效性核查和执行的措施等问题进行广泛的先行谈判。而现在提出的冻结实际上不可能进行核查。这样一种努力会使我们完全偏离目前正在进行的，达成实质性削减的谈判。

几年前，我在加利福尼业州一个人数众多的集会上听到一位年轻人的演讲。他是位年轻的父亲并且在娱乐圈名声大噪。在冷战期间，共产主义和我们自己的生活方式成为许多人萦绕心头的一个问题。当时他所谈的就是这个题目。突然，我听到他说："我爱我的女儿们胜过一切。"我自言自语道："哦，别那么说。你不能那么说，别说那个。"但是我低估了他。他接着说道："但我宁可看到我的孩子们现在怀着对上帝的信念阆然长逝，也不愿她们在共产主义的阴影下成长，并且有朝一日带着对上帝无所信仰的心态死去。"

听众当中有上千名年轻人，他们站起身来欢呼雀跃。他们立即就明白了那位父亲的话中所包含的深刻真理，即物质与精神何者是真正重要的。

让我们为所有那些生活于极权主义黑幕中的人祈祷。祝愿他们发现认识上帝的喜乐。但是在他们认识上帝之前，我们必须警觉，只要他们继续鼓吹国家的至高无上，宣扬国家对于个体的万能，并预言它将最终统治全人类，他们就是现代世界的邪恶中心。

刘易斯在他令人难忘的《地狱来鸿》中写道："当今最大的邪恶，并非是在狄更斯所热衷描绘的肮脏的罪恶之窟中炮制出来的，它甚至不是在集中营和劳改营犯下的，那些地方只是邪恶发作的最终结果。当今最大的邪恶是在整洁豪华、温暖明亮的办公室里构思和安排的；是由那些衣着光鲜、言谈斯文的人鼓动、支持、散布和记录的。

结果，由于这些人言谈斯文，由于他们有时流利自如地畅谈手足之情与和平，由于他们能像某些以前的独裁者一样总是在"最后才提出领土要求"，一些人就会要求我们相信他们的表白并且顺从他们的非份之想。但是，如果历史教会了我们，对对手一味妥协或一厢情愿实属愚不可及。它意味着背叛我们的过去，虚掷我们的自由。

因此，我敦促你们大声反对那些将美国置于军事和道德劣等地位的人士。我一直相信你们这些教会人士才是鲁益师书中那个老魔鬼的眼中钉。因此，在你们讨论核冻结提议时，我要提醒你们谨防傲慢的诱惑，那是一种洋洋自得地宣称自己凌驾于一切之上，并对双方各打五十大板的诱惑。它无视一个邪恶帝国的历史和勃勃野心，径自宣布军备竞赛不过是一场巨大的误会，由此而使自己游离于对与错、善与恶之外。

本届政府在尽力使美国保持强大和自由。当我们正在为真正和切实地削减核武库，并在上帝的帮助下最终彻底消灭核武器而进行谈判时，有些人会使你们撤回对我们努力的支持，我请求你们抵制这种诱惑。

虽然美国的军事实力是重要的，但我在这里要补充一点：我始终确信，当前为世界而进行的抗争从来不取决于炸弹或火箭，也不取决于军队或军事力量。我们今天所面临的真正危机是精神上的，从根本上说，是对道德意志和信仰的检验。

惠特克·钱伯斯，这位希斯·钱伯斯间谍案中的主角，以其自身的变节，见证了我们时代可怕创伤的人曾写道："某种程度上，西方世界的危机在于人们对上帝的漠视，从而配合了共产主义将人与神疏离开来的尝试。"他又说道："马列主义实际上是人类第二种最为古老的信仰，第一种信仰则是伊甸园中的诱惑之音：'你们会像神一样。'"

西方世界能够回应这种挑战，他写道："但这只有假定西方对上帝及天赋自由的信念与共产主义对人的信念一样伟大才行。"

我相信我们能够迎接这种挑战。我相信共产主义是人类历史上一个悲惨而诡异的篇章，即使这一章已经临近终结。我相信这是因为我们探求自由的力量源泉不是物质上的，而是精神上的。而且由于它是无尽的，所以必然对那些奴役同类的人形成威慑，并最终战胜他们。因为以赛亚书中写道："疲乏的，他赐予气力；无力的，他给予力量。但那些仰望主的人，必重新获得力量；他们必像鹰一样展翅上腾；他们奔跑，决不疲倦。"

改变你们的世界。我们的国父之一潘恩曾说："我们拥有重塑世界的内在力量。"我们能做到这一点，让我们同心协力来完成这项仅凭一己之力无法完成的事业。

愿上帝保佑你们，谢谢大家。

第三节　精彩语录

There are a great many God-fearing, dedicated, noble men and women in public life, present company included. And yes, we need your help to keep us ever-mindful of the ideas and the principles that brought us into the public arena in the first place. The basis of those ideals and principles is a commitment to freedom and personal liberty that, itself is grounded in the much deeper realization that freedom prospers only where the blessings of God are avidly sought and humbly accepted.

许许多多担任公职的人都是敬畏上帝、甘于奉献、品格高贵的人。我们需要你们的帮助，以使我们得以铭记那些将我们第一次带入政治舞台的理念与原则。这些理念与原则的基础是对自由和个人权利的信守，而这种信守本身又是建立在深刻的体察上。即只有在热切探求和谦卑地领受上帝祝福的地方，自由才会繁荣兴旺。

I'm pleased to be here today with you who are keeping America great by keeping her good. Only through your work and prayers and those of millions of others can we hope to survive this perilous century and keep alive this experiment in liberty, this last, best hope of man.

今天能与你们这些通过保持美国人的虔诚而使美国继续伟大的人士相聚，我感到非常愉快。只有通过你们和其他成千上万人的工作和祈祷，才能使我们在这个危机四伏的世纪有望幸存下来，并使自由这一人类最美好的希望生机勃勃。

Change your world. One of our Founding Fathers, Thomas Paine, said, "We have it within our power to begin the world over again." We can do it, doing together what no one church could do by itself.

改变你们的世界。我们的国父之一潘恩曾说："我们拥有重塑世界的内在力量。"我们能做到这一点，让我们同心协力来完成这项仅凭一己之力无法完成的事业。

第五章

推倒这堵墙

第一节 背景介绍

二战时期，德国纳粹疯狂挑起战争，不断扩张给欧洲甚至全球造成了巨大的灾难。随着二战反法西斯联盟的胜利，作为二战的战败国德国接受了国际联盟的惩罚。战胜国美英法苏把德国分成四个占领区，首都柏林由四个战胜国共管，苏联管辖东柏林。

1949 年在德国和柏林西部的美英法占领区建立了实行民主的德意志联邦共和国，简称西德。10 月 7 日在苏联占领区内也相应地成立了德意志民主共和国，即由共产党统治实行社会主义的东德。西柏林成为共产主义体制包围之中的自由之岛。

进入 20 世纪 50 年代后，由美英法占领的西德创造了战后的"经济奇迹"，发展突飞猛进，经济实力迅猛增长。而东德却由于背负着巨额的苏联战争赔款，以及强制实行计划经济，国民经济日渐衰退。东德与西德之间的经济实力差距越来越大。

1953 年 6 月 17 日东柏林百姓走上街头，要求自由选举，却遭到了苏联官方的反对。面对游行的群众，苏联派出坦克血腥镇压了这次民主运动。当时的政治强压与专制，使东德人民向往西德的自由世界。从此人们纷纷逃离东德。苏联和东德政府想方设法围堵逃亡的潮流，并为了这一目的修建了震惊世界的"柏林墙"。

1961 年 8 月 13 日清晨，当柏林市民一觉醒来时，突然发现西柏林四周筑起了一道高达 3.6 米到 4 米的屏障，全长约 170 公里，随后东德政府又进一步封闭了通往西德的边境。政府禁止任何人逾越柏林墙。

在长达几十年的隔离中，众多民众想尽办法越过这堵墙，有的是为了更自由的生活，有的则是为了与亲人团聚。在东德的强烈镇压下，成功的人寥寥无几。

德国的象征勃兰登堡门位于国会大厦 300 米开外。女武神在城门上傲视柏林城，与菩提树下大街另一端的亚历山大广场电视塔沉默地对峙。造访柏林的政治家都会来勃兰登堡门，冷战时代更是如此，因为这里正是东西德裂痕中最炽烈的伤口。

1987 年 6 月 12 日清晨，美国总统里根抵达柏林，此时这座城市正在庆贺其 750 岁诞辰。在将东西柏林割裂数年的分界线勃兰登堡门的柏林墙前，里根发表了著名的演讲。演讲稿由秘书起的草，听者主要是正意欲与美国缔结友好关系的苏联领导人米哈伊尔·戈尔巴乔夫，还有届时在场的两万名听众。因为担心会有恐怖袭击，里根身后放置了两块巨大的防弹玻璃。

在这次著名的演讲中，里根呼吁戈尔巴乔夫拆掉柏林墙，这一言辞遭到美国国务院和国家安全委员会的强烈反对，他们担心克里姆林宫的强硬派会以此向戈氏提出质疑。

里根总统在演讲中说出了震撼世界的话："戈尔巴乔夫总书记，

如果你要寻求和平，如果你要为苏联和东欧寻求繁荣，如果你要寻求自由，就来到这扇门前吧！戈尔巴乔夫先生，打开这扇门！戈尔巴乔夫先生，拆掉这堵墙！"

第二节 里根于 1987 年在柏林墙下的演讲

Thank you very much.

Chancellor Kohl, Governing Mayor Diepgen, ladies and gentlemen: Twenty-four years ago, President John F. Kennedy visited Berlin, speaking to the people of this city and the world at the City Hall. Well, since then two other presidents have come, each in his turn, to Berlin. And today I, myself, make my second visit to your city.

We come to Berlin, we American presidents, because it's our duty to speak, in this place, of freedom. But I must confess, we're drawn here by other things as well: by the feeling of history in this city, more than 500 years older than our own nation; by the beauty of the Grunewald and the Tiergarten; most of all, by your courage and determination. Perhaps the composer Paul Lincke understood something about American presidents. You see, like so many presidents before me, I come here today because wherever I go, whatever I do: Ich hab noch einen Koffer in Berlin. I still have a

suitcase in Berlin.

Our gathering today is being broadcast throughout Western Europe and North America. I understand that it is being seen and heard as well in the East. To those listening throughout Eastern Europe, a special word: Although I cannot be with you, I address my remarks to you just as surely as to those standing here before me. For I join you, as I join your fellow countrymen in the West, in this firm, this unalterable belief: Es gibt nur ein Berlin.

Behind me stands a wall that encircles the free sectors of this city, part of a vast system of barriers that divides the entire continent of Europe. From the Baltic, south, those barriers cut across Germany in a gash of barbed wire, concrete, dog runs, and guard towers. Farther south, there may be no visible, no obvious wall. But there remain armed guards and checkpoints all the same—still a restriction on the right to travel, still an instrument to impose upon ordinary men and women the will of a totalitarian state. Yet it is here in Berlin where the wall emerges most clearly; here, cutting across your city, where the news photo and the television screen have imprinted this brutal division of a continent upon the mind of the world. Standing before the Brandenburg Gate, every man is a German, separated from his fellow men. Every man is a Berliner, forced to look upon a scar.

President von Weizsacker has said, "The German question is open as long as the Brandenburg Gate is closed." Today I say: As long as the gate is closed, as long as this scar of a wall is permitted to stand, it is not the German question alone that remains open, but the question of freedom for all mankind. Yet I do not come here to lament. For I find in Berlin a message of hope, even in the shadow of this wall, a message of triumph.

In this season of spring in 1945, the people of Berlin emerged from their air-raid shelters to find devastation. Thousands of miles away, the people of the United States reached out to help. And in 1947 Secretary of State—as you've been told—George Marshall announced the creation of what would become known as the Marshall Plan. Speaking precisely 40 years ago this month, he said: "Our policy is directed not against any country or doctrine, but against hunger, poverty, desperation, and chaos."

In the Reichstag a few moments ago, I saw a display commemorating this 40th anniversary of the Marshall Plan. I was struck by the sign on a burnt-out, gutted structure that was being rebuilt. I understand that Berliners of my own generation can remember seeing signs like it dotted throughout the western sectors of the city. The sign read simply: "The Marshall Plan is helping here to strengthen the free world." A strong, free world in the West, that dream became real. Japan rose from ruin to become an economic giant. Italy, France, Belgium—virtually every nation in Western Europe saw political and economic rebirth; the European Community was founded.

In West Germany and here in Berlin, there took place an economic miracle, the Wirtschaftswunder. Adenauer, Erhard, Reuter, and other leaders understood the practical importance of liberty— that just as truth can flourish only when the journalist is given freedom of speech, so prosperity can come about only when the farmer and businessman enjoy economic freedom. The German leaders reduced tariffs, expanded free trade, lowered taxes. From 1950 to 1960 alone,

the standard of living in West Germany and Berlin doubled.

Where four decades ago there was rubble, today in West Berlin there is the greatest industrial output of any city in Germany—busy office blocks, fine homes and apartments, proud avenues, and the spreading lawns of parkland. Where a city's culture seemed to have been destroyed, today there are two great universities, orchestras and an opera, countless theaters, and museums. Where there was want, today there is abundance—food, clothing, and automobiles—the wonderful goods of the Kudamm. From devastation, from utter ruin, you Berliners have, in freedom, rebuilt a city that once again ranks as one of the greatest on earth. The Soviets may have had other plans. But my friends, there were a few things the Soviets didn't count on— Berliner Herz, Berliner Humor, jaund Berliner Schnauzer.

In the 1950s, Khrushchev predicted: "We will bury you." But in the West today, we see a free world that has achieved a level of prosperity and well-being unprecedented in all human history. In the Communist world, we see failure, technological backwardness, declining standards of health; even want of the most basic kind— too little food. Even today, the Soviet Union still cannot feed itself. After these four decades, then, there stands before the entire world one great and inescapable conclusion: Freedom leads to prosperity. Freedom replaces the ancient hatreds among the nations with comity and peace. Freedom is the victor.

Now the Soviets themselves may, in a limited way, be coming to understand the importance of freedom. We hear much from Moscow about a new policy of reform and openness. Some political prisoners have been released. Certain foreign news broadcasts are no longer being jammed. Some economic enterprises have been permitted to operate with greater freedom from state control.

Are these the beginnings of profound changes in the Soviet state? Or are they token gestures, intended to raise false hopes in the West, or to strengthen the Soviet system without changing it? We welcome change and openness; for we believe that freedom and security go together, that the advance of human liberty can only strengthen the cause of world peace.

There is one sign the Soviets can make that would be unmistakable, that would advance dramatically the cause of freedom and peace. General Secretary Gorbachev, if you seek peace, if you seek prosperity for the Soviet Union and Eastern Europe, if you seek liberalization: Come here to this gate! Mr. Gorbachev, open this gate! Mr. Gorbachev, tear down this wall!

I understand the fear of war and the pain of division that afflict this continent—and I pledge to you my country's efforts to help overcome these burdens. To be sure, we in the West must resist Soviet expansion. So we must maintain defenses of unassailable strength. Yet we seek peace; so we must strive to reduce arms on both sides.

Beginning 10 years ago, the Soviets challenged the Western alliance with a grave new threat, hundreds of new and more deadly SS-20 nuclear missiles, capable of striking every capital in Europe. The Western alliance responded by committing itself to a counter-deployment unless the Soviets agreed to negotiate a better solution; namely, the elimination of such weapons on both sides. For many months, the Soviets refused to bargain in earnestness. As the alliance, in turn, prepared to go forward with its counter-deployment, there

were difficult days—days of protests like those during my 1982 visit to this city—and the Soviets later walked away from the table.

But through it all, the alliance held firm. And I invite those who protested then—I invite those who protest today—to mark this fact: Because we remained strong, the Soviets came back to the table. And because we remained strong, today we have within reach the possibility, not merely of limiting the growth of arms, but of eliminating, for the first time, an entire class of nuclear weapons from the face of the earth.

As I speak, NATO ministers are meeting in Iceland to review the progress of our proposals for eliminating these weapons. At the talks in Geneva, we have also proposed deep cuts in strategic offensive weapons. And the Western allies have likewise made far-reaching proposals to reduce the danger of conventional war and to place a total ban on chemical weapons.

While we pursue these arms reductions, I pledge to you that we will maintain the capacity to deter Soviet aggression at any level at which it might occur. And in cooperation with many of our allies, the United States is pursuing the Strategic Defense Initiative—research to base deterrence not on the threat of offensive retaliation, but on defenses that truly defend; on systems, in short, that will not target populations, but shield them. By these means, we seek to increase the safety of Europe and all the world. But we must remember a crucial fact: East and West do not mistrust each other because we are armed; we are armed because we mistrust each other. And our differences are not about weapons but about liberty. When President Kennedy spoke at the City Hall those 24 years ago, freedom was encircled, Berlin was under siege. And today, despite all the pressures upon this city, Berlin stands secure in its liberty. And freedom itself is transforming the globe.

In the Philippines, in South and Central America, democracy has been given a rebirth. Throughout the Pacific, free markets are working miracle after miracle of economic growth. In the industrialized nations, a technological revolution is taking place—a revolution marked by rapid, dramatic advances in computers and telecommunications.

In Europe, only one nation and those it controls refuse to join the community of freedom. Yet in this age of redoubled economic growth, of information and innovation, the Soviet Union faces a choice: It must make fundamental changes, or it will become obsolete.

Today thus represents a moment of hope. We in the West stand ready to cooperate with the East to promote true openness, to break down barriers that separate people, to create a safe, freer world. Surely, there is no better place than Berlin, the meeting place of East and West, to make a start.

Free people of Berlin: Today, as in the past, the United States stands for the strict observance and full implementation of all parts of the Four Power Agreement of 1971. Let us use this occasion, the 750th anniversary of this city, to usher in a new era, to seek a still fuller, richer life for the Berlin of the future. Together, let us maintain and develop the ties between the Federal Republic and the Western sectors of Berlin, which is permitted by the 1971 agreement.

And I invite Mr. Gorbachev: Let us work to bring the Eastern and Western parts of the city closer together, so that all the inhabitants of all Berlin can enjoy the benefits that come with life in one of the great

cities of the world.

To open Berlin still further to all Europe, East and West, let us expand the vital air access to this city, finding ways of making commercial air service to Berlin more convenient, more comfortable, and more economical. We look to the day when West Berlin can become one of the chief aviation hubs in all central Europe.

With our French and British partners, the United States is prepared to help bring international meetings to Berlin. It would be only fitting for Berlin to serve as the site of United Nations meetings, or world conferences on human rights and arms control or other issues that call for international cooperation.

There is no better way to establish hope for the future than to enlighten young minds, and we would be honored to sponsor summer youth exchanges, cultural events, and other programs for young Berliners from the East. Our French and British friends, I'm certain, will do the same. And it's my hope that an authority can be found in East Berlin to sponsor visits from young people of the Western sectors.

One final proposal, one close to my heart: Sport represents a source of enjoyment and ennoblement, and you may have noted that the Republic of Korea—South Korea—has offered to permit certain events of the 1988 Olympics to take place in the North. International sports competitions of all kinds could take place in both parts of this city. And what better way to demonstrate to the world the openness of this city than to offer in some future year to hold the Olympic games here in Berlin, East and West?

In these four decades, as I have said, you Berliners have built a great city. You've done so in spite of threats—the Soviet attempts to impose the East-mark, the blockade. Today the city thrives in spite of the challenges implicit in the very presence of this wall. What keeps you here? Certainly, there is a great deal to be said for your fortitude, for your defiant courage. But I believe there's something deeper, something that involves Berlin's whole look and feel and way of life—not mere sentiment.

No one could live long in Berlin without being completely disabused of illusions. Something instead, that has seen the difficulties of life in Berlin but chose to accept them, that continues to build this good and proud city in contrast to a surrounding totalitarian presence that refuses to release human energies or aspirations. Something that speaks with a powerful voice of affirmation, that says yes to this city, yes to the future, yes to freedom.

In a word, I would submit that what keeps you in Berlin is love—love both profound and abiding. Perhaps this gets to the root of the matter, to the most fundamental distinction of all between East and West. The totalitarian world produces backwardness because it does such violence to the spirit, thwarting the human impulse to create, to enjoy, to worship. The totalitarian world finds even symbols of love and of worship an affront.

Years ago, before the East Germans began rebuilding their churches, they erected a secular structure: the television tower at Alexander Platz. Virtually ever since, the authorities have been working to correct what they view as the tower's one major flaw, treating the glass sphere at the top with paints and chemicals of every kind. Yet even today when the sun strikes that sphere—that sphere

that towers over all Berlin—the light makes the sign of the cross. There in Berlin, like the city itself, symbols of love, symbols of worship, cannot be suppressed.

As I looked out a moment ago from the Reichstag, that embodiment of German unity, I noticed words crudely spray-painted upon the wall, perhaps by a young Berliner: "This wall will fall. Beliefs become reality." Yes, across Europe, this wall will fall. For it cannot withstand faith; it cannot withstand truth. The wall cannot withstand freedom.

And I would like, before I close, to say one word. I have read, and I have been questioned since I've been here about certain demonstrations against my coming.

And I would like to say just one thing, and to those who demonstrate so. I wonder if they have ever asked themselves that if they should have the kind of government they apparently seek, no one would ever be able to do what they're doing again.

Thank you and God bless you all.

非常感谢。

科尔总理、迪普根市长、女士们、先生们：二十四年前约翰·卜.肯尼迪总统访问了柏林，在市政厅向本市和全世界的人民发表了讲话。从那以后另两位总统也访问了柏林，而今天我自己也开始了我的第二次访问。

我们这些美国总统来到柏林，是因为我们有责任到这里为自由呼吁。但是我也必须承认，我们之所以来到这里，还有其他的原因。这个城市历史悠久，比我的国家还要古老五百年；格鲁内瓦尔德和蒂尔加滕优美瑰丽，引人入胜；而最主要的原因是，我被你们的勇气和决心所打动。作曲家保罗·林克也许同我们这些美国总统有着共鸣。你们瞧，就像我之前的许多总统一样，我今天来到这里是因为我无论走到哪里，无论我干什么：Ich hab noch einen Koffer in Berlin（我还有个箱子在柏林）。

今天，我们的集会正被整个西欧和北美现场直播，我也知道在东方也能被看见被听到。对于那些正在聆听的东欧人民，我有一句特别的话要说：虽然我不能和你们在一起，但是我对你们讲的话就和对那些站在我面前的人民所讲的一样，我同你们以及你们西方的同胞一样，都有一个坚定的、不可变更的信念：只有一个柏林！

在我的身后，有一个包围着本市的所谓自由之墙，它是一个将全欧洲分割的巨大邪恶系统的一部分。一堵从波罗的海绵延到南方的无形之墙，这个壁垒横裂德国，处处扎满铁丝网，浇筑混凝土，军犬和全副武装的军人巡逻不休，警戒塔密布。或许在更远的南方，我们可能不会看见一堵明显的墙，但是那里仍然有着武装的警卫和关卡！在墙的那边，一个极权国家仍然在残酷地控制着他的人民，没有旅行，不能出国，言论不自由。然而，没有哪个地方比柏林更能感受到这种区别了。正是在这里，新闻图片和电视屏幕都在全世界人民的心上烙刻着这道横贯你们的城市，分裂整个大陆的伤痕。每一个站在勃兰登堡门前的人都是德国人，被迫同自己的骨肉同胞分离。每一个人都是柏林人，被迫俯视那道伤痕。

冯·魏茨泽克总统曾经说过："只要勃兰登堡门还关闭着，德国的问题就将存在。"今天我要说："只要这道门还关闭着，只要这堵墙的伤痕仍然允许存在，那么长存的就不仅仅只是德国人自己的问题，还有整个人类的自由问题。我来这里绝不是为了哀悼，因

为我在柏林找到了一个希望，即使在这堵墙的阴影之下，仍然有着胜利的消息。

在 1945 年春季，当柏林人民步出空袭避难所时，他们发现的是一片狼藉，数千英里之外的美国人民伸出了援助之手。在 1947 年，正如你们知道的那样，美国国务卿乔治·马歇尔宣布了被称之为"马歇尔计划"的援助方案。四十年前的今天，他说："我们的政策不针对任何国家、任何主义，我们针对的是饥饿、贫穷、绝望和混乱。"

稍早的时候，在德国国会大厦，我参观了一个纪念马歇尔计划四十周年的展览。在一个曾被熔毁正在重建的建筑物上，我看到了一条标语，这条标语深深地打动了我。我知道，我这一代的柏林人都还记得，在西柏林曾经遍布着这样的标语。这个标语是："为加强自由世界，马歇尔计划在这里伸出援手。"在西方，一个强大自由的世界，一个伟大的自由梦想正在成真。日本从废墟中崛起成为一个经济巨人，意大利、法兰西、比利时，几乎每一个西欧国家都见证了政治上和经济上的复兴，欧共体也得以诞生。

在西德，在柏林发生了经济奇迹，the Wirtschaftswunder（德国奇迹）。阿登纳、埃哈德、路透等领导人深知自由在实践上的重要意义；只有当新闻记者被赋予言论自由之时，真相才会浮现；只有农民和商人能够享受到经济自由的时候，繁荣才会到来。德国领导人削减关税，扩大自由贸易，降低税率。仅仅在 1950 年到 1960 年十年间，西德和西柏林的生活水准就成倍翻升。

在西柏林，四十年前还是一片废墟的地方，现在是德国产出最大的工业区，到处是繁忙的办公区、优良的住宅和公寓、热闹的大街和不断蔓延的公园草坪。在当年似乎是文化荒漠的地方，现在有两所最好的大学、乐团和一家歌剧院，无数的剧场和博物馆。过去物资极度匮乏，现在有丰富的食品、服装和汽车，在库达姆大街上应有尽有。在废墟上，从毁灭处，你们这些柏林人在自由中重建了地球上最伟大的城市之一。苏联人或许有其他的计划，但是我的朋友们，有些东西却是苏联人永远没有的，那就是柏林人的心灵、柏林人的幽默和柏林人的雪纳瑞。

在20世纪50年代，赫鲁晓夫曾预言："我们将埋葬你们"。但是在今天的西方，我们看到的是一片前所未有的繁荣和安宁。而在共产主义世界，我们看见了失败，看见了技术上的落后，看见了健康的倒退，看见了即使连最起码的东西——食品都极度匮乏的情形！即使到了今天，苏联人仍然不能喂饱自己。在四十年之后的今天，在整个世界面前，耸立着一个伟大和必然的结论：自由导致繁荣，自由用礼让和宽容代替了各国之间古老的仇恨。自由是胜利者！

现在苏联人自己可能在某种程度上，也明白了自由的重要性。我们经常从莫斯科听到一些消息，一项改革和开放的新政策已经出台，一些政治犯已经得到释放，某些外国新闻广播不再被屏蔽，一些经济企业已经被允许拥有更多的自主权。

这些举动是苏联发生巨大转变的开始吗？或者他们仅仅是做出姿态，想要在西方掀起错误的希望，又或者仅仅是企图在不更改苏联体制的前提下修修补补？我们欢迎变化和开放，因为我们相信自由和安全相伴，人类自由的进步只会加强世界的和平。

这里有一件事是苏联人可以做出来而不至于遭到误解的，这件事将里程碑式的促进人类自由和和平的事业。戈尔巴乔夫总书记，如果你真的在寻求和平，如果你真的在寻求苏联和东欧的繁荣昌盛，如果你真的在寻求自由，那么，来到这扇门前吧。戈尔巴乔夫先生，

打开这扇门吧！戈尔巴乔夫先生，推倒这堵墙吧！

我理解战争的恐惧、分离的痛苦折磨着这片大陆，我向你们保证，我的国家会帮助克服这些障碍。为了万无一失，我们自由世界必须抵抗苏联的扩张，因此我们必须保持牢不可破的防御力量。然而我们也在寻求和平，因此我们也必须做出努力来削减双方的军备。

从十年之前开始，苏联人带来了一种新的致命威胁挑战着西方联盟，他们部署了数百枚更新式、更致命的SS-20核导弹，这些导弹足以摧毁欧洲的每一个都市。西方联盟则以相应的部署以牙还牙，除非苏联人同意进行谈判，找到一个更好的解决方式，也就是双方共同消除这样的武器，否则局面只能这么僵持下去。这么多月以来，那些苏联人一直拒绝进行诚实的谈判，作为联盟我们一方准备进行相应部署。那些困难的日子让我想起，我在1982年访问这座城市时，许多人举行抗议，并且苏联人稍后离开了谈判桌。

但尽管有这些困难，我们的联盟仍然坚持住了。我邀请那时抗议的那些人，我邀请今天抗议的这些人来注意这样一个事实，那就是因为我们的强硬，苏联人最后又回到了谈判桌上；因为我们的强硬，今天我们能做到的，不仅仅只是期望限制军备的增长，而且还包括这样一种可能，那就是将核武器彻底地从地球上废除掉。

当我讲话时，北约的部长们正在冰岛会晤，对这一建议的进展状况进行讨论。在日内瓦会谈中，我们也提出了要对战略进攻性武器进行大的削减。西方联盟已经提出了许多内容深广的提议来减少发生常规战争的危险，以及彻底禁绝化学武器。

当我们裁减这些军备的时候，我也向你们保证，我们将保持能力，以阻止苏联在任何层次上发动侵略。我们正在同许多盟友合作，对"战略防御构想"计划进行研究，不是将威慑构建于威胁报复之上，而是着眼于真正的防御。简而言之，这套防御体系将不瞄准平民，而是保护他们。通过这种方式，欧洲和全世界的安全将得以增强。但是我们必须牢记一个至关重要的事实：东方和西方不敢轻举妄动，是因为我们势均力敌；而我们势均力敌，又是因为我们彼此猜疑。使东西方意见不同的不是武器本身，而是对自由的不同理解。肯尼迪总统二十四年前在市政厅演讲时，自由被包围，柏林在围困之中。然而今天，尽管敌人对这个城市施加了那么多压力，柏林仍然安全的沐立在自由之光下，自由本身也在改变着整个世界。

在菲律宾、在南美和中美洲，民主已经获得重生。在整个太平洋地区，自由市场正在制造一个又一个经济增长的奇迹。在工业化国家，一次技术革命正在发生，这次技术革命的标志是计算机和电信方面的迅速发展。

在欧洲，只有一个国家和它控制的那些卫星国拒绝加入自由阵营，然而在这个经济成倍增长的时代中，在这个信息与革新的时代中，苏联面临着一个选择：它必须进行根本的改变，否则它将变得过时。

因此，今天就代表着希望。我们西方准备好与东方进行合作，促进真正的开放，打破分离人们的藩篱，建立一个安全和自由的世界。我想没有哪个地方比柏林，这个连接东西方人民的地方，更适合作为一个起点。

柏林的自由人民们，美国今天会像过去一样，坚定地捍卫人类的自由和尊严，无论前面的道路有多么凶险，无论极权者有多么的虚伪。让我们借这个机会，本市的 750 周年纪念日，迎接一个新的时代，建设一个更加充实、更加富裕的柏林。让我们维护并发展联邦德国与西柏林之间的联系，这是 1971 年协议所允许的。

　　并且我将邀请戈尔巴乔夫先生：让我们一起为东西柏林的人民做点事情吧，使他们靠得更紧一点，使整个柏林的居民都能享受到生活在这个世界上最伟大的都市之一所带来的乐趣。

　　要进一步向整个欧洲、东方和西方开放柏林，我们就要扩展进入这个城市的重要空中通道，使通向柏林的商业航空服务更便利、更舒适，也更经济。我们期待着有一天西柏林可以成为整个中欧地区的主要航空枢纽之一。

　　同我们的法国和英国同伴一起，美国准备在柏林召开各种国际会议。对柏林这个城市来说，召开联合国会议或者有关人权、军备控制等，需要国际合作议题的国际会议，是再合适不过的。

　　要为将来带来希望，没有比点亮青年人心灵更好的方法。我们将极为荣幸地赞助（东西柏林的）夏季青年交流、各类文化活动，以及为东柏林青年举办的其他活动。我敢肯定我们法国和英国的朋友也将这样做。我也希望东柏林当局能够赞助西柏林青年的访问活动。

　　我心中最后一个建议是，运动是快乐与高贵之源。大家可能会注意到，南韩已经允许1988年夏季奥运会的某些赛事在北方举行。各种国际体育比赛也可以在这个城市的两个部分举行。假如在将来的某一年，奥林匹克运动会能够在柏林——东柏林与西柏林举行，那么还有什么更好的方式，比这更能向世界展示柏林这个城市的开放呢？

　　在这四十年中，正如我所说，你们柏林人建立了一个伟大的城市。尽管存在着许多威胁——苏联所强加的关口和封锁，你们还是做到了。尽管有这堵墙所隐喻着的挑战，这个城市仍然蓬勃发展。是什么使你们坚持下来？当然有许多原因，比如，你们的毅力，你们抵抗的勇气。

但是我相信有些原因更加深邃，涉及的是柏林整体的精神面貌、感受和生活方式，而不仅仅只是情操。

长期生活在柏林没有人还能心存幻想，他们看到了柏林生活的困难，但选择接受之。尽管被囚禁着人类活力和希望的极权主义制度所包围，他们仍然继续建设着这个美好、令人自豪的城市。那是一种强有力的声音，这种声音对这座城市，对未来，对自由大声说："是。"

简而言之，我会把这种东西称之为"爱"——深刻而持久的爱。也许这就是问题的根源，这就是东西方之间最根本的区别。极权主义的世界生产落后，因为它侵犯这种精神，阻碍了人类去创造、去享受、去感悟的冲动。极权主义的世界，甚至觉得爱和宗教的符号是一种侮辱。

几年前，当东德开始重建自己的教堂之前，他们建设了一个世俗的建筑物：亚历山大广场电视塔。自那以后，东德当局一直在努力纠正（在他们眼中）该塔的一个重大缺陷，往其顶部的玻璃球上倾倒各种涂料和化学物品。然而直到今天，每当阳光照射到这些玻璃上，还是能照射出十字架的摸样。在这里，在柏林，爱的符号，礼拜的符号不会受到压制。

当我之前从国会大厦，这个德国统一的化身往外望的时候，我看到柏林墙上一段喷漆的话，这可能是一个年轻的柏林人写下来的："这堵墙终将倒下，梦想终将成为现实。"在整个欧洲，这堵墙终将倒下，因为它经不起良知的考验，经不起真理的追问，经不起自由的期望！

在我结束演讲之前，我还要多说几句。自从我来到这里就已经知道，也被人问起过，关于某些团体抗拒我到来的事情。

　　我想对那些示威者说，我不知道他们是否想过，如果他们确实建立了他们所希望的那种政府，就不会有人能够做他们现在正在做的这些事情了。

　　谢谢大家，上帝会保佑你们的。

第三节 精彩语录

Behind me stands a wall that encircles the free sectors of this city, part of a vast system of barriers that divides the entire continent of Europe. From the Baltic, south, those barriers cut across Germany in a gash of barbed wire, concrete, dog runs, and guard towers. Farther south, there may be no visible, no obvious wall. But there remain armed guards and checkpoints all the same—still a restriction on the right to travel, still an instrument to impose upon ordinary men and women the will of a totalitarian state. Yet it is here in Berlin where the wall emerges most clearly; here, cutting across your city, where the news photo and the television screen have imprinted this brutal division of a continent upon the mind of the world. Standing before the Brandenburg Gate, every man is a German, separated from his fellow men. Every man is a Berliner, forced to look upon a scar.

在我的身后，有一个包围着本市的所谓自由之墙，它是一个将全欧洲分割的巨大邪恶系统的一部分。一堵从波罗的海绵延到南方的无

形之墙，这个壁垒横裂德国，处处扎满铁丝网，浇筑混凝土，军犬和全副武装的军人巡逻不休，警戒塔密布。或许在更远的南方，我们可能不会看见一堵明显的墙，但是那里仍然有着武装的警卫和关卡！在墙的那边，一个极权国家仍然在残酷地控制着他的人民，没有旅行，不能出国，言论不自由，然而，没有哪个地方比我们柏林更能感受到这种区别了，正是在这里，新闻图片和电视屏幕在全世界人民的心上烙刻着这道横贯你们的城市，分裂整个大陆的伤痕。每一个站在勃兰登堡门前的人都是德国人，被迫同自己的骨肉同胞分离。每个人是一名柏林人，被迫俯视那惨痛的伤痕。

Adenauer, Erhard, Reuter, and other leaders understood the practical importance of liberty—that just as truth can flourish only when the journalist is given freedom of speech, so prosperity can come about only when the farmer and businessman enjoy economic freedom.

阿登纳、埃哈德、路透等领导人深知自由在实践上的重要意义：只有当新闻记者被赋予言论自由之时，真相才会浮现；只有农民和商人能够享受到经济自由的时候，繁荣才会到来。

After these four decades, then, there stands before the entire world one great and inescapable conclusion: Freedom leads to prosperity. Freedom replaces the ancient hatreds among the nations with comity and peace. Freedom is the victor.

在四十年之后的今天，在整个世界面前，耸立着一个伟大和必然的结论：自由导致繁荣，自由用礼让和宽容代替了各国之间古老的仇恨。自由是胜利者！

Today thus represents a moment of hope. We in the West stand ready to cooperate with the East to promote true openness, to break down barriers that separate people, to create a safe, freer world. Surely, there is no better place than Berlin, the meeting place of East and West, to make a start.

因此，今天就代表着希望。我们西方准备好与东方进行合作，促进真正的开放，打破分离人们的藩篱，建立一个安全和自由的世界。我想没有哪个地方比柏林，这个连接东西方人民的地方，更适合作为一个起点。

"This wall will fall. Beliefs become reality. " Yes, across Europe, this wall will fall. For it cannot withstand faith; it cannot withstand truth. The wall cannot withstand freedom.

"这堵墙终将倒下，梦想终将成为现实。"在整个欧洲，这堵墙终将倒下，因为它经不起良知的考验，经不起真理的追问，经不起自由的期望！

第六章

抉择的时刻

第一节 背景介绍

1964年，里根作了一场题为《抉择的时刻》的演讲，以帮助共和党总统候选人、参议员巴里·戈德华特竞选成功。他在讲话中说："我们必须捍卫自由，否则自由将离我们而去。"这句话成为当年风靡美国的名言。

这番精彩的电视讲话成为他人生中的一个转折点，使他从此开始了政治上的辉煌生涯。里根于1966年当选为加州州长，并于1970年连任。随着"水门"丑闻的曝光，里根的政治声望更是与日俱增。1976年，他在挑战尼克松"钦定"继承人杰拉尔德·R.福特时，仅以60票的微弱劣势惜败给对手，结果福特当选第三十八任美国总统。

虽然那次演讲十分成功，可巴里最终还是输给了对手，1965年入主白宫的是民主党人约翰逊总统。

巴里·戈德华特获得总统提名的道路并不平坦。在巴里·戈德华特角逐共和党提名总统选举之时，共和党分裂为保守派（来自西

部和中西部）与自由派（来自东北部）。巴里·戈德华特毫不妥协
的财政保守主义以及强硬的反共主义，使一些较温和的共和党人对
他抱持疑虑。他被传统的共和党人视为太过于右派的政治光谱，并
且认为他不能吸引主流的选民以赢得大选。因此自由派的共和党人
抬出了一系列的候选人以对抗巴里·戈德华特，包括纽约州的州长
纳尔逊·洛克菲勒等人。巴里·戈德华特在加利福尼亚州的初选中
成功击败洛克菲勒，接着赢得了共和党提名。他同时也受到南部共
和党人的坚定支持。

在 1964 年共和党全国代表大会上发表接受总统选举提名的演
讲中，巴里·戈德华特大胆的宣誓道："捍卫自由时的极端并不是
罪恶，追求正义时的温和并不是美德。"这一段来自西塞罗的演讲
词是由哈利·雅法所提议的，演讲稿则是由卡尔·海丝所撰写。由
于总统林登·约翰逊的高昂人气，巴里·戈德华特在选战中避免直
接地攻击约翰逊，他在代表大会上甚至没有直接提到过约翰逊。

性格决定命运，巴里·戈德华特的保守与强硬让他在选战中备受
挑剔。选战中巴里·戈德华特在过去的失言也都被挖了出来，他曾经
称艾森豪威尔总统是新政的廉价版本，艾森豪威尔也一直对此耿耿于
怀。不过艾森豪威尔还是与巴里·戈德华特一起拍了一段电视的竞选
广告，在 11 月艾森豪威尔表示他会在大选中投票给共和党，间接地
表示了他对于巴里·戈德华特的最终肯定。在 1961 年 12 月巴里·戈
德华特曾在记者会上宣称道："有时候我真觉得，如果我们可以把整
个西海岸割开，让它们飘到海里，这个国家会变得更好。"这段发言
后来被约翰逊阵营挖出，以此猛烈攻击巴里·戈德华特。巴里·戈德
华特主张将社会福利自愿化以及将田纳西河谷管理局（一个大型的新
政机构）拍卖掉的发言也都引起类似的争议。

里根为了替巴里·戈德华特阵营造势，发表了一段知名的全国电视演讲《抉择的时刻》，以支持巴里·戈德华特。演说取得了不错的效果，这段演讲的成功，促使里根在 1966 年投入竞选加利福尼亚州州长，并且开启了他之后的政治生涯。约翰逊阵营的文宣将巴里·戈德华特描绘为一个危险的极端份子。约翰逊在 1964 年民主党全国代表大会的演讲中，也没有直接提及巴里·戈德华特的名字。

在竞选的过程中，每个竞选者都极力避免犯错，而每个错误都极有可能影响自己的政治前途。巴里·戈德华特主张的强硬反共外交政策，被约翰逊及其竞选阵营用作攻击他的把柄，宣称巴里·戈德华特的好战性格会导致灾难性的结果甚至是核战争。在越战议题上巴里·戈德华特批评约翰逊的政策完全缺乏目标、方向或决心，并且导致在丛林中的大量死亡和自由的逐步毁灭。巴里·戈德华特在核战争议题上的言论，则被许多人视为是毫不妥协，这种印象又被巴里·戈德华特的一些失言所加深。例如，他曾说："我们应该扔一颗（核弹）到克里姆林宫的厕所里去。"

巴里·戈德华特尽力抵挡约翰逊阵营的攻击，批评约翰逊政府在一些道德议题上的缺失，并且在一则竞选广告中宣称："……我们身为一个国家，已经离那种可以导致国破家亡的道德腐败境界不远了……现在正是将良心重新竖回政府的时候，以此为榜样，使其重现美国生活的每个角落……"

在 1964 年选举期间，以揭发丑闻为主的杂志 Fact 出版了一期特别刊号，标题为《一个保守派的无良心：揭露巴里·戈德华特的心理状态》。文章里宣称巴里·戈德华特的精神状况不适合担任总统，并举出一则对精神病医师进行民调的结果为证据：Fact 杂志邮寄测验给 12,356 位精神病医师，并且公布其中 2,417 名医师回复的抽样结果，其中 1,189 人认为巴里·戈德华特不适合担任总统。在选举过后，巴里·戈德华特控告杂志的发行者、杂志编辑以及杂志社毁谤罪，虽然最初陪审团只判给巴里·戈德华特 1 美元的名誉赔偿费，但是后来的上诉则使巴里·戈德华特从杂志社获得 50,000 美元的赔偿。

在共和党全国代表大会上，来自全国各地的候选人和大量的新闻记者、州代表团、州党部代表以及各式各样的人物充斥会场，使 1964 年的全国代表大会弥漫着一股紧张而又充满敌意的气氛。

选举的结果，巴里·戈德华特只获得了 38.4% 的选票，在选举人团上只赢得六个州，获得了 52 张选举人团票，而约翰逊则一面倒地赢得了 486 张。巴里·戈德华特在选后还曾坦率地说："这场选举即使是亚伯拉罕·林肯回来替我们竞选，我们也是输定了。"

巴里·戈德华特的惨败，加上当时大多数选民都有总统票同国会票（亦即死忠支持与他们总统选票候选人相同政党的国会候选人）的习惯，当年的国会选举中共和党也遭受大败，许多在位已久的老牌国会议员都在此年选举中被击败。

晚年时巴里·戈德华特曾宣称，如果不是因为当年全国都还沉浸在总统约翰·肯尼迪被刺杀后的悲伤气氛里，使选民对于连续两年便更换三位总统有所顾虑，他的确有机会赢得选举。许多人也常举出巴里·戈德华特在当年选举里赢下了许多南方的州，在那之前美国南部一向都是民主党的地盘。1964 年的这次选举也预见了在未来几十年里，美国政治光谱的转变，美国南部从那时开始便逐渐向共和党倾斜，从总统选举开始，到最后国会和州的地方选举都成了共和党称霸的局面。

虽然巴里·戈德华特对于美国保守主义的影响，还不及 1965 年

以后的罗纳德·里根，从 1950 年末到 1964 年之间，是巴里·戈德华特一手定义，并且开拓了美国后几十年的保守主义运动。亚利桑那州的参议员约翰·麦凯恩谈到巴里·戈德华特时说道："他将共和党从原本一个由东部菁英组织主导的组织，转变为后来可以让里根一路走向总统选举的环境。"政治评论家乔治·威尔在谈到 1980年的美国总统选举时也说："1964 年的选举花了整整十六年时间才开完票，而巴里·戈德华特最后赢了。"

第二节 里根于 1964 年为总统候选人助选的演讲

Thank you. Thank you very much. Thank you and good evening. The sponsor has been identified, but unlike most television programs, the performer hasn't been provided with a script. As a matter of fact, I have been permitted to choose my own words and discuss my own ideas regarding the choice that we face in the next few weeks.

I have spent most of my life as a Democrat. I recently have seen fit to follow another course. I believe that the issues confronting us cross party lines. Now, one side in this campaign has been telling us that the issues of this election are the maintenance of peace and prosperity. The line has been used, "We've never had it so good."

But I have an uncomfortable feeling that this prosperity isn't something on which we can base our hopes for the future. No nation in history has ever survived a tax burden that reached a third of its national income.Today, 37 cents out of every dollar earned in this country is the tax collector's share, and yet our government continues

to spend 17 million dollars a day more than the government takes in. We haven't balanced our budget 28 out of the last 34 years. We've raised our debt limit three times in the last twelve months, and now our national debt is one and a half times bigger than all the combined debts of all the nations of the world. We have 15 billion dollars in gold in our treasury; we don't own an ounce. Foreign dollar claims are 27.3 billion dollars. And we've just had announced that the dollar of 1939 will now purchase 45 cents in its total value.

As for the peace that we would preserve, I wonder who among us would like to approach the wife or mother whose husband or son has died in South Vietnam and ask them if they think this is a peace that should be maintained indefinitely. Do they mean peace, or do they mean we just want to be left in peace? There can be no real peace while one American is dying some place in the world for the rest of us.

We're at war with the most dangerous enemy that has ever faced mankind in his long climb from the swamp to the stars, and it's been said if we lose that war, and in so doing lose this way of freedom of ours, history will record with the greatest astonishment that those who had the most to lose did the least to prevent its happening. Well I think it's time we ask ourselves if we still know the freedoms that were intended for us by the Founding Fathers.

Not too long ago, two friends of mine were talking to a Cuban refugee, a businessman who had escaped from Castro, and in the midst of his story one of my friends turned to the other and said, "We don't know how lucky we are." And the Cuban stopped and said, "How lucky you are? I had someplace to escape to." And in that sentence he told us the entire story. If we lose freedom here, there's no place to escape to. This is the last stand on earth.

And this idea that government is beholden to the people, that it has no other source of power except the sovereign people, is still the newest and the most unique idea in all the long history of man's relation to man.

This is the issue of this election: whether we believe in our capacity for self-government or whether we abandon the American revolution and confess that a little intellectual elite in a far-distant capitol can plan our lives for us better than we can plan them ourselves.

You and I are told increasingly we have to choose between a left or right. Well I'd like to suggest there is no such thing as a left or right. There's only an up or down: man's old—old-aged dream, the ultimate in individual freedom consistent with law and order, or down to the ant heap of totalitarianism. And regardless of their sincerity, their humanitarian motives, those who would trade our freedom for security have embarked on this downward course.

In this vote-harvesting time, they use terms like the "Great Society," or as we were told a few days ago by the President, we must accept a greater government activity in the affairs of the people. But they've been a little more explicit in the past and among themselves; and all of the things I now will quote have appeared in print.

These are not Republican accusations. For example, they have voices that say, "The cold war will end through our acceptance of a not undemocratic socialism." Another voice says, "The profit motive has become outmoded. It must be replaced by the incentives of the

welfare state." Or, "Our traditional system of individual freedom is incapable of solving the complex problems of the 20th century."

Senator Fulbright has said at Stanford University that the Constitution is outmoded. He referred to the President as "our moral teacher and our leader," and he says he is "hobbled in his task by the restrictions of power imposed on him by this antiquated document." He must "be freed," so that he "can do for us" , what he knows "is best."

And Senator Clark of Pennsylvania, another articulate spokesman, defines liberalism as "meeting the material needs of the masses through the full power of centralized government."

Well, I, for one, resent it when a representative of the people refers to you and me, the free men and women of this country, as "the masses." This is a term we haven't applied to ourselves in America.

But beyond that, "the full power of centralized government" —this was the very thing the Founding Fathers sought to minimize. They knew that governments don't control things. A government cannot control the economy without controlling people. And they know when a government sets out to do that; it must use force and coercion to achieve its purpose. They also knew, those Founding Fathers, that outside of its legitimate functions, government does nothing as well or as economically as the private sector of the economy.

Now, we have no better example of this than government's involvement in the farm economy over the last 30 years. Since 1955, the cost of this program has nearly doubled. One-fourth of farming in America is responsible for 85% of the farm surplus. Three-fourths of farming is out on the free market and has known a 21% increase in the per capita consumption of all its produce. You see, that one-fourth of farming—that's regulated and controlled by the federal government. In the last three years, we've spent 43 dollars in the feed grain program for every dollar bushel of corn we do not grow.

Senator Humphrey last week charged that Barry Goldwater, as President, would seek to eliminate farmers. He should do his homework a little better, because he'll find out that we've had a decline of 5 million in the farm population under these government programs. He will also find that the Democratic administration has sought to get from Congress extension of the farm program to include those three-fourths that is now free. He'll find that they've also asked for the right to imprison farmers who wouldn't keep books as prescribed by the federal government.

The Secretary of Agriculture asked for the right to seize farms through condemnation and resell them to other individuals. And contained in that same program was a provision that would have allowed the federal government to remove 2 million farmers from the soil.

At the same time, there's been an increase in the Department of Agriculture employees. There's now one for every 30 farms in the United States, and still they can't tell us how 66 shiploads of grain headed for Austria disappeared without a trace and Billie Sol Estes never left shore.

Every responsible farmer and farm organization has repeatedly asked the government to free the farm economy, but how—who are farmers to know what's best for them? The wheat farmers voted against a wheat program. The government passed it anyway. Now the

price of bread goes up; the price of wheat to the farmer goes down.

Meanwhile, back in the city, under urban renewal the assault on freedom carries on. Private property rights so diluted that public interest is almost anything a few government planners decide it should be. In a program that takes from the needy and gives to the greedy, we see such spectacles as in Cleveland, Ohio, a million–and–a–half–dollar building completed only three years ago must be destroyed to make way for what government officials call a "more compatible use of the land." The President tells us he's now going to start building public housing units in the thousands, where heretofore we've only built them in the hundreds.

But FHA （Federal Housing Authority）and the Veterans Administration tell us they have 120,000 housing units they've taken back through mortgage foreclosure. For three decades, we've sought to solve the problems of unemployment through government planning, and the more the plans fail, the more the planners plan. The latest is the Area Redevelopment Agency.

They've just declared Rice County, Kansas, a depressed area. Rice County, Kansas, has two hundred oil wells, and the 14,000 people there have over 30 million dollars on deposit in personal savings in their banks. And when the government tells you you're depressed, lie down and be depressed.

We have so many people who can't see a fat man standing beside a thin one without coming to the conclusion the fat man got that way by taking advantage of the thin one. So they're going to solve all the problems of human misery through government and government planning. Well, now, if government planning and welfare had the answer—and they've had almost 30 years of it—shouldn't we expect government to read the score to us once in a while? Shouldn't they be telling us about the decline each year in the number of people needing help? The reduction in the need for public housing?

But the reverse is true. Each year the need grows greater; the program grows greater. We were told four years ago that 17 million people went to bed hungry each night. Well that was probably true. They were all on a diet. But now we're told that 9.3 million families in this country are poverty-stricken on the basis of earning less than 3,000 dollars a year. Welfare spending 10 times greater than in the dark depths of the Depression.

We're spending 45 billion dollars on welfare. Now do a little arithmetic, and you'll find that if we divided the 45 billion dollars up equally among those 9 million poor families, we'd be able to give each family 4,600 dollars a year. And this added to their present income should eliminate poverty. Direct aid to the poor, however, is only running only about 600 dollars per family. It would seem that someplace there must be some overhead.

Now—so now we declare "war on poverty," or "You, too, can be a Bobby Baker." Now do they honestly expect us to believe that if we add 1 billion dollars to the 45 billion we're spending, one more program to the 30-odd we have—and remember, this new program doesn't replace any, it just duplicates existing programs—do they believe that poverty is suddenly going to disappear by magic? Well, in all fairness I should explain there is one part of the new program that isn't duplicated. This is the youth feature.

We're now going to solve the dropout problem, juvenile

delinquency, by reinstituting something like the old CCC camps, and we're going to put our young people in these camps. But again we do some arithmetic, and we find that we're going to spend each year just on room and board for each young person we help 4,700 dollars a year. We can send them to Harvard for 2,700! Course, don't get me wrong. I'm not suggesting Harvard is the answer to juvenile delinquency.

But seriously, what are we doing to those we seek to help? Not too long ago, a judge called me here in Los Angeles. He told me of a young woman who'd come before him for a divorce. She had six children, was pregnant with her seventh. Under his questioning, she revealed her husband was a laborer earning 250 dollars a month. She wanted a divorce to get an 80 dollar raise. She's eligible for 330 dollars a month in the Aid to Dependent Children Program. She got the idea from two women in her neighborhood who'd already done that very thing.

Yet anytime you and I question the schemes of the do-gooders, we're denounced as being against their humanitarian goals. They say we're always "against" things—we're never "for" anything.

Well, the trouble with our liberal friends is not that they're ignorant; it's just that they know so much that isn't so.

Now—we're for a provision that destitution should not follow unemployment by reason of old age, and to that end we've accepted Social Security as a step toward meeting the problem.

But we're against those entrusted with this program when they practice deception regarding its fiscal shortcomings, when they charge that any criticism of the program means that we want to end payments to those people who depend on them for a livelihood.

They've called it "insurance" to us in a hundred million pieces of literature. But then they appeared before the Supreme Court and they testified it was a welfare program. They only use the term "insurance" to sell it to the people. And they said Social Security dues are a tax for the general use of the government, and the government has used that tax.

There is no fund, because Robert Byers, the actuarial head, appeared before a congressional committee and admitted that Social Security as of this moment is 298 billion dollars in the hole. But he said there should be no cause for worry because as long as they have the power to tax, they could always take away from the people whatever they needed to bail them out of trouble. And they're doing just that.

A young man, 21 years of age, working at an average salary—his Social Security contribution would, in the open market, buy him an insurance policy that would guarantee 220 dollars a month at age 65. The government promises 127. He could live it up until he's 31 and then take out a policy that would pay more than Social Security.

Now are we so lacking in business sense that we can't put this program on a sound basis, so that people who do require those payments will find they can get them when they're due—that the cupboard isn't bare?

Barry Goldwater thinks we can.

At the same time, can't we introduce voluntary features that would permit a citizen who can do better on his own to be excused upon presentation of evidence that he had made provision for the

non-earning years?

Should we not allow a widow with children to work, and not lose the benefits supposedly paid for by her deceased husband? Shouldn't you and I be allowed to declare who our beneficiaries will be under this program, which we cannot do?

I think we're for telling our senior citizens that no one in this country should be denied medical care because of a lack of funds. But I think we're against forcing all citizens, regardless of need, into a compulsory government program, especially when we have such examples, as was announced last week, when France admitted that their Medicare program is now bankrupt. They have come to the end of the road.

In addition, was Barry Goldwater so irresponsible when he suggested that our government give up its program of deliberate, planned inflation, so that when you do get your Social Security pension, a dollar will buy a dollar's worth, and not 45 cents worth?

I think we're for an international organization, where the nations of the world can seek peace. But I think we're against subordinating American interests to an organization that has become so structurally unsound that today you can muster a two-thirds vote on the floor of the General Assembly among nations that represent less than 10 percent of the world's population.

I think we're against the hypocrisy of assailing our allies because here and there they cling to a colony, while we engage in a conspiracy of silence and never open our mouths about the millions of people enslaved in the Soviet colonies in the satellite nations.

I think we're for aiding our allies by sharing of our material blessings with those nations which share in our fundamental beliefs, but we're against doling out money government to government, creating bureaucracy, if not socialism, all over the world. We set out to help 19 countries. We are helping 107.

We've spent 146 billion dollars. With that money, we bought a 2 million dollar yacht for Haile Selassie. We bought dress suits for Greek undertakers, extra wives for Kenya government officials. We bought a thousand TV sets for a place where they have no electricity.

In the last six years, 52 nations have bought 7 billion dollars worth of our gold, and all 52 are receiving foreign aid from this country.

No government ever voluntarily reduces itself in size. Therefore, governments' programs, once launched, never disappear. Actually, a government bureau is the nearest thing to eternal life we'll ever see on this earth.

Federal employees—federal employees number two and a half million; and federal, state, and local, one out of six of the nation's work force employed by government. These proliferating bureaus with their thousands of regulations have cost us many of our constitutional safeguards. How many of us realize that today federal agents can invade a man's property without a warrant? They can impose a fine without a formal hearing, let alone a trial by jury? And they can seize and sell his property at auction to enforce the payment of that fine.

In Chico County, Arkansas, James Wier over-planted his rice allotment. The government obtained a 17,000 dollar judgment. And a U.S. marshal sold his 960-acre farm at auction. The government said

it was necessary as a warning to others to make the system work.

Last February 19th at the University of Minnesota, Norman Thomas, six-times candidate for President on the Socialist Party ticket, said, "If Barry Goldwater became President, he would stop the advance of socialism in the United States." I think that's exactly what he will do.

But as a former Democrat, I can tell you Norman Thomas isn't the only man who has drawn this parallel to socialism with the present administration, because back in 1936, Mr. Democrat himself, Al Smith, the great American, came before the American people and charged that the leadership of his Party was taking the Party of Jefferson, Jackson, and Cleveland down the road under the banners of Marx, Lenin, and Stalin. And he walked away from his Party, and he never returned til the day he died—because to this day, the leadership of that Party has been taking that Party, that honorable Party, down the road in the image of the labor Socialist Party of England.

Now it does not require expropriation or confiscation of private property or business to impose socialism on a people. What does it mean whether you hold the deed to the—or the title to your business or property if the government holds the power of life and death over that business or property? And such machinery already exists.

The government can find some charge to bring against any concern it chooses to prosecute. Every businessman has his own tale of harassment. Somewhere a perversion has taken place. Our natural, unalienable rights are now considered to be a dispensation of government, and freedom has never been so fragile, so close to slipping from our grasp as it is at this moment.

Our Democratic opponents seem unwilling to debate these issues. They want to make you and I believe that this is a contest between two men—that we're to choose just between two personalities.

Well what of this man that they would destroy—and in destroying, they would destroy that which he represents, the ideas that you and I hold dear? Is he the brash and shallow and trigger-happy man they say he is? Well I've been privileged to know him "when." I knew him long before he ever dreamed of trying for high office, and I can tell you personally I have never known a man in my life I believed so incapable of doing a dishonest or dishonorable thing.

This is a man who, in his own business before he entered politics, instituted a profit-sharing plan before unions had ever thought of it. He put in health and medical insurance for all his employees. He took 50 percent of the profits before taxes and set up a retirement program, a pension plan for all his employees. He sent monthly checks for life to an employee who was ill and couldn't work. He provides nursing care for the children of mothers who work in the stores. When Mexico was ravaged by the floods in the Rio Grande, he climbed in his airplane and flew medicine and supplies down there.

An ex-GI told me how he met him. It was the week before Christmas during the Korean War, and he was at the Los Angeles airport trying to get a ride home to Arizona for Christmas. And he said that there were a lot of servicemen there and no seats available on the planes. And then a voice came over the loudspeaker and said, "Any men in uniform wanting a ride to Arizona, go to runway such-and-such," and they went down there, and there was a fellow named Barry Goldwater sitting in his plane. Every day in those weeks before

Christmas, all day long, he'd load up the plane, fly it to Arizona, fly them to their homes, fly back over to get another load.

During the hectic split-second timing of a campaign, this is a man who took time out to sit beside an old friend who was dying of cancer. His campaign managers were understandably impatient, but he said, "There aren't many left who care what happens to her. I'd like her to know I care."

This is a man who said to his 19-year-old son, "There is no foundation like the rock of honesty and fairness, and when you begin to build your life on that rock, with the cement of the faith in God that you have, then you have a real start."

This is not a man who could carelessly send other people's sons to war. And that is the issue of this campaign that makes all the other problems I've discussed academic, unless we realize we're in a war that must be won.

Those who would trade our freedom for the soup kitchen of the welfare state have told us they have a utopian solution of peace without victory. They call their policy "accommodation". And they say if we'll only avoid any direct confrontation with the enemy, he'll forget his evil ways and learn to love us. All who oppose them are indicted as warmongers.

They say we offer simple answers to complex problems. Well, perhaps there is a simple answer—not an easy answer—but simple: If you and I have the courage to tell our elected officials that we want our national policy based on what we know in our hearts is morally right.

We cannot buy our security, our freedom from the threat of the bomb by committing an immorality so great as saying to a billion human beings now enslaved behind the Iron Curtain, "Give up your dreams of freedom because to save our own skins, we're willing to make a deal with your slave masters." Alexander Hamilton said, "A nation which can prefer disgrace to danger is prepared for a master, and deserves one." Now let us set the record straight.

There is no argument over the choice between peace and war, but there's only one guaranteed way you can have peace—and you can have it in the next second—surrender.

Admittedly, there's a risk in any course we follow other than this, but every lesson of history tells us that the greater risk lies in appeasement, and this is the specter our well-meaning liberal friends refuse to face—that their policy of accommodation is appeasement, and it gives no choice between peace and war, only between fight or surrender.

If we continue to accommodate, continue to back and retreat, eventually we have to face the final demand—the ultimatum. And what then—when Nikita Khrushchev has told his people he knows what our answer will be? He has told them that we're retreating under the pressure of the Cold War, and someday when the time comes to deliver the final ultimatum, our surrender will be voluntary, because by that time we will have been weakened from within spiritually, morally, and economically. He believes this because from our side he's heard voices pleading for "peace at any price" or "better Red than dead," or as one commentator put it, he'd rather "live on his knees than die on his feet." And therein lies the road to war, because those voices don't speak for the rest of us.

You and I know and do not believe that life is so dear and peace so sweet as to be purchased at the price of chains and slavery. If nothing in life is worth dying for, when did this begin—just in the face of this enemy?

Or should Moses have told the children of Israel to live in slavery under the pharaohs? Should Christ have refused the cross? Should the patriots at Concord Bridge have thrown down their guns and refused to fire the shot heard 'round the world? The martyrs of history were not fools, and our honored dead who gave their lives to stop the advance of the Nazis didn't die in vain. Where, then, is the road to peace? Well it's a simple answer after all.

You and I have the courage to say to our enemies, "There is a price we will not pay." "There is a point beyond which they must not advance." And this—this is the meaning in the phrase of Barry Goldwater's "peace through strength." Winston Churchill said, "The destiny of man is not measured by material computations. When great forces are on the move in the world, we learn we're spirits—not animals." And he said, "There's something going on in time and space, and beyond time and space, which, whether we like it or not, spells duty."

You and I have a rendezvous with destiny.

We'll preserve for our children this, the last best hope of man on earth, or we'll sentence them to take the last step into a thousand years of darkness.

We will keep in mind and remember that Barry Goldwater has faith in us. He has faith that you and I have the ability and the dignity and the right to make our own decisions and determine our own destiny.

Thank you very much.

谢谢，非常感谢。晚上好。主办单位找到了。但不同于大多数的电视节目，这里不给演员提供台词。因此，我可以用自己的话来说说，我怎样来看待数周后的选举。

我这辈子大部分时间都是民主党。最近，我才感到我比较适合另一套路子。我认为我们面临的问题是跨党派的。如今，一边的阵营在告诉我们，本轮选举的议题是维护和平与繁荣。这话说的，"我们没法再好了。"

但是我觉得不妥。这个"繁荣"不是我们所希望的未来。历史上没有任何国家，在税负高到国民所得的三分之一，还可以活着的。如今，每赚1美元就有37美分要上交国库作为税收。而我们的政府每天超支1,700万美元。过去三十四年，有二十八年预算没有平衡过。在过去的一年时间里，我们已经把债务上限提高了3倍。如今，我们国家的债务是全世界国家债务总和的1.5倍。我们的国库只有150亿元的黄金，但1盎司都不属于我们，外国货币占去了273亿。而我们刚刚说，现在1美元的购买力只相当于1939年的45美分。

说到我们要和平，我想知道，我们中间有没有人去了解那些妻子和母亲们，他们的丈夫和孩子在南越牺牲了。你问问他们，这是否是该无条件维护的和平。他们意味着和平吗？还是意味着我们只想要在"和平"中度日而已？如果还有一位美国人在世界某处为我们大家牺牲，就不可能有真正的和平。

我们遭遇的是人类有史以来最险恶的敌人。据说如果我们输掉战争，我们的自由也将如此失去。历史将会有这样震惊的记载，那

些人之所以一败涂地，因为他们连最起码的阻挡也没有做过。我想该是我们扪心自问的时候了，我们是否依然知悉建国先贤为我们开创的自由道路。

不久前，我的两位朋友和一个古巴难民聊天，他是从卡斯特罗那里逃出来的生意人。当古巴人述说他的遭遇时，其中一个朋友对另一个说："我们不知道我们有多幸运。"古巴人停了下来说："你们有多幸运？我只要有个地方可以躲就行了。"他的这句话说明了一切。如果我们这里也失去了自由，那全世界都无处可逃了。这是地球上最后的自由之地。

政府理应为人民服务，因为权力是至高的人民所授予的，除此之外，没有其他的来源。在人与人关系的历史长河中，这种理念仍然是最新、最独特的。

本轮选举的主题是：我们要相信自我管理的能力，还是摒弃美国革命的理念，承认偏远的国会里有一小撮精英可以为我们的生活作计划，而且计划得比我们更好。

越来越多的人像你我一样，要求我们选左派或右派。我想提议的是，别管什么左派右派。这里只有向上派或向下派：向上，是人类古老的梦想，是个体自由的目标，它与法律和秩序是一致的。所谓向下，就是像蚁群一样，甘愿自己被极权主义压在底层，不管真心诚意也好，或是出于人道主义也罢，他们都会以安全为由，出卖我们的自由，走上这条向下沉沦的道路。

在这个争夺选票的时刻，他们说"伟大社会"这番话，要不就像前几天总统和我们讲，我们必须接受"政府进一步对于民事的干预"。而过去他们还含糊其辞，模棱两可。我说的所有这一切，你们都能在报纸上看见。

这些不是共和党的指控。比如，他们说："如果我们接受不民主的社会主义，冷战就结束了。"还有人说："争夺利润的激励制度已经过时了。应该由福利国家的激励机制来取代。"或者，"我们个人自由的传统体制无法解决 20 世纪的复杂问题"。

参议员富布赖特在斯坦福大学说，宪法已经过时了。他说，总统是"我们的道德导师，是我们的领袖。他说，他的工作被这篇限制权力的'古文'束缚了。应该给他'自由'，让他尽心为我们做他认为最好的事情。"

还有一位发言人，宾夕法尼亚州参议员克拉克，他直截了当把"自由主义"定义为："通过集权政府的所有权力来满足民众的物质需求。"

作为民众之一，我不喜欢这样的说法。因为议员说的所谓"民众"，是指你、我以及我们国家所有自由的男人和女人。在美国，"民众"这样的词，我们自己已不适用了。

除此之外，"集权政府的所有权力"是建国先贤极力避免的。他们知道，政府无法控制事情。一个政府要控制经济，必然要压制人民。他们知道如果政府要这样做，必须通过暴力和强制的手段来实现。那些建国先贤，他们当然知道，政府除立法职能之外，在经济上的作为，完全不如私有经济领域。

我们用过去三十年政府干预农业的例子来说明问题是再好不过了。从 1955 年以来，这项计划的成本增加了将近一倍。美国 85%的农产品过剩是由四分之一的农业（政府干预的那部分）造成的，除此之外，依靠自由市场的四分之三的农业，其农产品人均消费量增长了 21%。你看，这四分之一的农业——是由联邦政府来规范和控制的。在过去的三年，我们的饲料粮计划，用 43 美元产不出 1

美元的玉米量。

参议员汉弗莱上周指控巴里·戈德华特是企图消灭农民的总统。他如果多做点功课的话就会发现，政府这些计划让我们的农业人口减少了 500 万。他也会发现，民主党政府在寻求国会支持将农场计划扩张到自由市场里四分之三的农业。他会发现，他们还要申请特权来关押那些不按照联邦政府规定来记账的农民。

农业部部长还要申请接管农场特权，通过没收农场并转售给其他人的手段。如果把这个条款放到同一个计划里，等于允许联邦政府把 200 万农民从土地上赶走。

与此同时，农业部却在增加雇员。如今，美国每三十个农民就有一个公务员来管，这些公务员无法向我们交代，去奥地利的六十六艘满载稻米的船怎么会消失得无影无踪？比利·索尔·埃斯蒂斯都没有出过海。

凡是负责任的农民和农场组织都一再要求过政府放弃对农业的管制，但是，除了农民自己，还有谁知道什么对他们有利呢？麦农投票反对麦子计划。政府照样通过该计划。现在，面包价格上涨，农民的小麦价格下跌。

与此同时，在城市里，所谓"重建市区"在侵害民众的自由。私有财产权被蚕食，所谓高于一切的"公共利益"，却由几位政府规划者说了算。政府的计划夺走贫困者的财产，送予贪心者享用。俄亥俄州克利夫兰就发生了这样不幸的事。三年前花了 150 万盖好的房子，因为政府要"让土地使用更具有兼容性"，就强制拆除。我们的总统说，那里要盖数千栋公共住宅，目前只有几百栋。

FHA（联邦房屋管理局）和退伍军人管理局说，他们已经收回了止赎的 12 万套住房。为了解决失业问题，政府搞了三十多年的计划，但是计划失败得越多，计划就越多。最新的是"地区再开发局"。

他们刚刚说堪萨斯州赖斯县是一个贫困地区。而堪萨斯州赖斯县有 200 口油井，14,000 人，他们在银行的个人存款超过 3,000 万。如果政府说你穷，那就你认了吧，穷就穷吧。

不是有人断言，胖子之所以肥是因为胖子揩了瘦子的油，我们很多人是看不到瘦子的边上还站着个胖子的。于是，他们打算通过政府和政府计划来解决人类所有的贫穷问题。如果政府的计划和福利真的是解药，那么他们搞了将近三十年福利，他们的成绩不该给我们看看吗？难道他们不该对我们说，需要帮助的人逐年在减少吗？需要住公共住宅的人也在下降吗？

但事实恰恰相反。每年穷人都在增加，而政府计划增长也越大。四年前，我们听政府说，每晚有 1,700 万人饿着肚子上床睡觉。说不定确有此事，他们都在节食。但是，现在我们又听说，我国有 930 万户年收入低于 3,000 美元的家庭，他们穷困潦倒。如今，福利开支是极度黑暗的大萧条时期的 10 倍。

我们的福利开支有 450 亿美元。你现在算算就会发现，如果我们把 450 亿元均分给 900 万户贫困家庭，每年每户家庭就能拿到 4,600 元。加上他们目前的收入，他们应该不穷了。但直接给到穷人手里的援助，每户家庭只有 600 元左右。这似乎意味着在别的什么地方开销用过了头。

现在，我们宣布"向贫困开战"，或者"你也可以是鲍比·贝克（国策顾问）"。他们真的要我们相信在 450 亿的开支上再加 10 亿，或者三十多个计划上再加一个计划，我们就能……记住，新计划不会改变什么，它只是复制现有的计划。说心里话，应该说在这个新计划中有一部分是不重复的。那是有关年轻人的部分。

我们现在又要搞老套的"公共资源保护队"计划，新政时期让青年铺路，植树，建公园，让年轻人入团来解决辍学问题和青少年犯罪问题。但是我们稍微计算一下就会发现，单单花在年轻人的吃住上，每年每人就要用掉 4,700 美元。花 2,700 元我们就可以把他们送进哈佛！当然，不要误解，我并不是说要哈佛来解决青少年犯罪的问题。

但是说真的，我们对那些需要帮助的人都做了些什么？不久前，洛杉矶的一个法官打电话给我，他说，有名年轻妇女到他那里要离婚。她生了六个孩子，肚子里还怀着第七个。在他的再三追问下才知道，她丈夫是名劳工，月收入 250 美元。她要离婚是想再得到 80 美元收入。因为按照援助抚养子女计划，她有资格每月享受 330 美元的补贴。她这么做是受到她两个邻居的启发，他们也都是这样做的。

然而，每当我们质疑这些良心人士的计划时，我们就被批评说我们反对的是人道主义的目标。他们说，我们总是"反对"一切，从来不会"支持"。

我们的左派朋友的问题不是他们太无知，而是他们知道得太多，且并非如此。

现在，我们支持这样的一个条款，所谓年老失业不应该是贫穷的借口，因此我们认为可将社会保障作为解决问题的第一步。

但是，我们反对那些计划受惠者钻财政的漏洞作弊骗钱，我们反对一听到批评政府计划，就指责其用心是让政府停止补助那些靠补贴才能度日的人。

在大量的文献中，他们称之为"保险"。而在最高法院，他们的呈词说这是一种"福利"计划。他们以"保险"的名义推销给老百姓。他们说"社保"费用是政府为了公共用途才征的税，而且政府已经用过了这些税。

政府的社保帐户上并没有钱。在国会委员会上，精算师罗伯特·拜尔斯承认，当时社保有2,980亿美元的缺口。但他说不要担心，只要政府还有权力征税，无论他们要什么，总能从老百姓那儿征收上来，问题便可迎刃而解了。目前，他们就是这么做的。

一个二十一岁的年轻人，如果他的工资达到平均水平，那么他缴的社会保障金，在公开市场上足够买到一份保险计划，保证他在六十五岁时每月领到220元。但政府只承诺将来给他127元。于是，他会等到三十一岁时，选择办一份比"社保"补偿更好的保险计划。

这样看来，我们政府是不是很没有商业头脑呢，这个计划根本靠不住。一旦到了社保兑现期，大家向政府要钱时，就会发现"这个橱柜不是空掉了吗？"

巴里·戈德华特认为我们能做到。

与此同时，我们可不可以推出一些自愿的条款，允许自己能做得更好的公民不加入政府计划，只要他能证明自己为退休时候做好了准备。

不准有小孩的寡妇上班，否则不给她抚恤金，我们这样做，对吗？按理她已故的丈夫也交过税？在这个计划中，你和我难道都没有权力决定自己的受益人是谁？我们不能做什么？

我认为我们不该因为缺钱而剥夺老年人享受医疗保险。但是，我们反对那种不管民众需不需要，都强制他们加入政府的计划。尤其我们还有前车之鉴。就在上周，法国宣布医保计划破产。这条路已经走到了尽头。

再者，巴里·戈德华特不负责任了吗？他建议我国政府停止搞

那种精心策划的人为的通货膨胀。这样将来你得到的养老金，1 美元还值 1 美元，而不是只值 45 美分？

我认为我们要支持一个让世界各国能够寻求和平的国际组织。但我们要反对凌驾于美国利益之上的组织，即便是获得了联合国大会三分之二的支持票。因为这个组织的结构不健全，它代表的人口还不到世界总人口的十分之一。

我认为我们要反对那种虚伪。一边抨击我们盟国，因为他们这儿或那儿还坚持着一个殖民地，一边却暗地里搞阴谋诡计，对苏联的殖民地，苏联卫星国中受奴役的千百万人三缄其口。

我认为我们要支持那些与我们志同道合的盟国，与他们分享我们的物资。而不是在各国政府之间乱捐钞票，这些国家不是搞社会主义就是在搞官僚主义。我们的目标是要帮助 19 个国家，但如今我们帮助了 107 个。

我们花费了 1,460 亿美元。这些钱我们让海尔·塞拉西买了 200 万的游艇，让希腊的殡仪官穿了礼服，让肯尼亚政府官员有了情妇，我们买了 1,000 台电视机，结果却送到一个连电都没有的地方。

过去的六年里，共有 52 个国家购买了我国的黄金，价值 70 亿美元。而这些国家全部都接受过我国的援助。

没有政府会主动缩减自身的规模。因此，政府的计划一经推出永不消失。其实，政府官僚机制是我们在地球上看到的最不容易灭绝的东西。

联邦雇员拥有 250 万之众，而本国六分之一的劳动力受雇于联邦、州与地方政府。这些官僚机构猛增，成千上万条的管制侵蚀了我们的宪政保障。究竟有多少人意识到，如今连逮捕证都不带的联邦特工就能私闯民宅？他们可以不经过正式听证而执行罚款，更不用说陪审团的判决机制了？他们可以通过查封和拍卖别人的财产来强制执行罚款。

在阿肯色州奇科县，詹姆斯·威尔种植水稻的用地超标了。于是，政府获得了 17,000 元的判罚。法院执行官把他 960 英亩的农场拍卖掉了。政府还说这非常必要，可以警告其他的人，让这个机制起作用。

去年二月在明尼苏达大学，诺曼·托马斯这位获得社会党六次提名的总统候选人说："如果巴里·戈德华特成为总统，他会停止美国走向极权的道路。"我想正是如此。

作为一个前民主党人，我告诉你们，不只是诺曼·托马斯把现政府比作社会主义。早在 1936 年，民主党人阿尔·史密斯，这个伟大的美国人，就曾在美国民众面前指控他的党领袖背离了杰斐逊、杰克逊和克利夫兰的路线，而跑到了反方的麾下。他退党了，直到死也没有回头。因为直到那一天，该党的领袖还在带领着这个光荣的党，沿着英格兰的劳工社会党的路线走下去。

现在都不用霸占或没收私有财产和企业，或对老百姓强制推行极权。什么意思呢？如果政府掌握了企业和财产的生杀大权，即使你拥有房契或者在自己公司做官，又有什么用呢？这种机制已经存在了。

政府随随便便就能找到一些罪名来控告你。凡是生意人都有过被骚扰的经历。有些地方莫名其妙的事也会发生。我们天赋的不可剥夺的权利，如今被认为是政府的一种特许，自由从未如此脆弱，几乎此刻就要从我们手中滑落。

我们民主党的对手似乎不愿意讨论这些问题。他们想要让你和我都相信这是两个男人在竞争，我们只需要根据两人的人品做出选

择而已。

那么，他们要在哪一点上击垮他（巴里·戈德华特）呢？击垮他所代表的理念，那是你和我都珍惜的理念。他是所谓的轻浮和浅薄，喜欢满嘴放炮的人吗？我有幸能够认识他，在他还没有参选之前，我早就认识他了。就我个人而言，我可以告诉你，我可以打保票他是最不会去做那种不诚实或不光彩的事的人。

在进入政坛之前，他有自己的公司。他制定了一项让员工分享利润的计划，这点他比工会想到得还要早。他为公司里的所有员工购买了健康和医疗保险。他把税前利润的50%用来为所有员工设立一项退休计划。他每月都送一位患病，无法上班的员工去检查身体。他给在店面工作的母亲提供儿童保育费。墨西哥的兰德河发洪水的时候，他驾驶自己的飞机为灾民送去药品和物资。

一名前海外军人告诉我，他见过巴里·戈德华特。那是在战争时期，某个圣诞节的前一周，他在洛杉矶亚利桑那州机场要搭飞机回家过圣诞节。他说，当时军人很多，飞机上已经没有多余的座位。这时，喇叭里传来了一个声音说："凡是想搭机去亚利桑那州的各位军人请去跑道。"于是，他们就下去了，有一个叫巴里·戈德华特的人在飞机里等他们。在圣诞节前几周，巴里·戈德华特每天都会过来，从早到晚地运送客人，送他们去亚利桑那州，送他们回家，然后飞回来，再运一次。

即使在这个分秒必争的选战时刻，他也会抽出时间去陪一位罹患癌症即将离世的老朋友。他的竞选经纪人很不理解，但是他（巴里·戈德华特）说："没有多少左派会在乎她。我想让她知道我在乎她。"

他曾对自己十九岁的儿子说："没有什么根基胜过诚实和公平

这样的磐石，你要把你的人生建在这块磐石之上，用你对上帝的信仰来加固，这才是你人生的真正起点。"

他并不是那种不停地怂恿别人孩子去打仗的人。选战的这个议题使我之前讨论过的问题显得不切实际，除非我们意识到这场战争我们一定要取得胜利。

那些人为了要福利国家的"流动厨房"而出卖我们的自由。他们对我们说，他们有乌托邦式的和平解决方案，用不着获得战争的胜利。他们称他们的政策为"和解"。他们说，如果我们能避免与敌人正面交锋，敌人就会放弃自己的罪恶活动，并且会逐渐喜欢我们。凡是反对他们方案的人都被他们指控为战争贩子。

他们说，我们为复杂的问题提供了简单的答案。也许有一个简单的答案，但是不容易做到，除非你和我鼓足勇气告诉当选的官员，我们希望国家政策在道义上是正确的，能对得起我们的良心。

我们不能为了自己的安全和自由不受炸弹的威胁，而出卖良心地对铁幕下饱受奴役的 10 亿人说："放弃你们的自由梦想吧，因为我们要明哲保身，我们要和你们的主子做交易。"亚历山大·汉密尔顿说："如果一个国家宁受屈辱也不愿意铤而走险，那么它在激请一个主子，活该被它奴役。"

现在，我们要以正视听。所谓要和平还是要战争都是空谈，想要那种打保票的和平，只有一个办法，而且立刻就能实现，那就是"投降"。

的确，除投降之外，我们任何的做法都有风险，但所有的历史教训都告诉我们，绥靖政策的风险更大。他们的和解政策就是绥靖政策，我们好心的自由派朋友们却回避了魔咒。和平与战争没得选，要么战斗，要么投降。

如果我们坚持和解，继续退让和撤退，最终我们不得不面对最后的命令，最后通牒。接着，赫鲁晓夫会告诉他的人，他知道我们会怎样反应？他会说我们因为迫于冷战的压力而撤兵了。某天到了下最后通牒的时候，我们会主动地投降，因为到那时我们在精神上、道义上、经济上都被削弱了。他如此确信，因为从我们这里他听到了恳求的声音"为了求和，不惜任何代价"或"宁可被共产，也不要死于核战"，或正如一位评论家所说的那样，他宁愿"跪着生，也不要死在他的脚下。"通往战争的道路就在那一点上，因为这些话不代表我们的声音。

你和我都知道，我们不相信"生命如此宝贵，和平如此甜美，以至于不惜以枷锁和奴役为代价去换取它们"。（出自帕特里克·亨利）难道生命中没有什么值得牺牲的，什么时候才开始这样，是因为面前有这样的敌人吗？

摩西应该告诉为奴的以色列人听命于法老吗？基督曾拒绝背负十字架吗？爱国的勇士们应该在康科德桥就把枪扔掉，不该打响惊动世界的那一枪吗？历史上的烈士不是笨蛋，我们这些光荣的逝者用他们的生命阻止了纳粹的扩张，他们没有白死。通往和平的道路在哪里？答案非常简单。

你和我鼓起勇气告诉我们的敌人："我们不买这个账。""有一点更为重要，就是他们必须停止扩张。"这就意味着，巴里·戈德华特的那句话："和平要靠实力。"温斯顿·丘吉尔说过："人的命运不是以物质积累来衡量的，当世界上伟大的军队在前进的时候，我们意识到我们是灵魂的人，而非动物。"他说："有件事正在时空或超时空中发生着，不管我们喜欢还是不喜欢，那叫做责任。"

命运让你和我走到一起。

为了我们的孩子，我们一定要保守住人类最后的憧憬，否则我们将会让他们跌入千年的黑暗。

我们要铭记，巴里·戈德华特有颗忠于我们的心。他相信，你和我都有能力，有尊严，有权利自己做决定，决定自己的命运。

非常感谢。

第三节 精彩语录

As for the peace that we would preserve, I wonder who among us would like to approach the wife or mother whose husband or son has died in South Vietnam and ask them if they think this is a peace that should be maintained indefinitely. Do they mean peace, or do they mean we just want to be left in peace? There can be no real peace while one American is dying some place in the world for the rest of us.

说到我们要和平，我想知道，我们中间有没有人去了解那些妻子和母亲们，他们的丈夫和孩子在南越牺牲了。你问问他们，这是否是该无条件维护的和平。他们意味着和平吗？还是意味着我们只想要在"和平"中度日而已？如果还有一位美国人在世界某处为我们大家牺牲，就不可能有真正的和平。

And this idea that government is beholden to the people, that it has no other source of power except the sovereign people, is still the newest and the most unique idea in all the long history of man's relation to man.

政府理应为人民服务，因为权力是至高的人民所授予的，除此之外，没有其他的来源。在人与人关系的历史长河中，这种理念仍然是最新、最独特的。

This is a man who said to his 19-year-old son, "There is no foundation like the rock of honesty and fairness, and when you begin to build your life on that rock, with the cement of the faith in God that you have, then you have a real start."

他曾对自己十九岁的儿子说"没有什么根基胜过诚实和公平这样的磐石，你要把你的人生建在这块磐石之上，用你对上帝的信仰来加固，这才是你人生的真正起点。"

We'll preserve for our children this, the last best hope of man on earth, or we'll sentence them to take the last step into a thousand years of darkness.

为了我们的孩子，我们一定要保守住人类最后的憧憬，否则我们将会让他们跌入千年的黑暗。

We will keep in mind and remember that Barry Goldwater has faith in us. He has faith that you and I have the ability and the dignity and the right to make our own decisions and determine our own destiny.

我们要铭记，巴里·戈德华特有颗忠于我们的心。他相信，你和我都有能力，有尊严，有权利自己做决定，决定自己的命运。

第七章

离去如此甜蜜而感伤

第一节 背景介绍

里根受任于美国的危难之秋，却带给了美国一个灿烂的春天。20世纪70年代初，美国爆发了1933年大萧条以来最大的经济危机，因数次中东战争导致的石油危机触发了严重的经济衰退，其明显病症是经济停滞不前，但通货膨胀使物价高企，失业率居高不下，社会矛盾激增。而从20世纪60年代初延至70年代久战不胜的越战，以及与前苏联持续胶着的冷战，也不断消蚀着人们对美国价值的认同感，重振经济雄风和重建美国精神成为亟待解决的问题。1981年1月，年已七十的罗纳德·威尔逊·里根就任美国第四十任总统。在美国政坛，里根创造了多个之最，他是唯一一位演员出身的总统，也是当选年龄最大且最长寿的总统，他还是第一位主张极权将会垮台的国家元首。他没有学过经济专业，却在最危难的时候带领美国走出滞胀泥潭，"里根经济学"成为世界经济史上一个响当当的学说。

20世纪三四十年代大萧条以来，凯恩斯经济学曾风行资本主义世界，其主张国家采用扩张性的经济政策，通过增加需求促进经济增长。到 20 世纪 70 年代，凯恩斯主张的增加政府开支实行赤字预算，增发公债、货币，降低利率等措施让滞胀程度有增无减，加剧了经济危机。当凯恩斯主义的神话难继时，里根决定反其道行之，凯恩斯主义向来强调供需中的"需求"，而里根经济学以"供应学派"为基础，强调"供应创造自身的需求"，目的就是减少税收，刺激经济，创造就业。为此，里根政府采取了一系列措施。

削减财政开支（不包括军费），尤其是"随意性"的社会福利开支。自罗斯福新政至二战后，美国建立了优越的社会保障制度，联邦政府机构也因此膨胀，据统计在 1965 年至 1980 年期间，联邦赤字增加了 53 倍，各种在联邦名义计划之下的救济款项增加了 4 倍，达到一年近 3,000 亿美元，联邦预算增加了约 5 倍，许多资金在行政管理中浪费掉。随着滞胀的到来，需要救济的人越来越多，问题也越来越严重。里根就职时说："政府并不是解决问题的方法，政府本身才是问题所在。"上台后，他大刀阔斧地进行了社会福利的改革。主要措施是：改变联邦政府过重的社会福利负担；大幅度削减社会福利保障支出，尤其是随意性开支；由州和地方政府更多地负担社会福利保障的责任。1983 年 4 月，里根签署了国会通过的一揽子社会福利改革计划，削减了一些社会保障项目，尤其是随意性的社会福利开支。在 1982~1985 财政年度，未成年儿童家庭补助和食品券开支比 1981 年减少 13%，医疗补助减少了 5%，儿童营养补助减少了 4.4%。由于紧缩了财政开支，联邦预算赤字从 1983 年的 1950 亿美元下降到 1984 年的 1,750 亿美元。

1981 年美国国会通过了里根政府提出的税法，要求从 1981 年 10 月起的三年内，分三次降低个人所得税，共减少个人所得税 23%，边际税率从 14%~70% 降为 11%~50%。1981~1984 年间联邦

政府税收减少了 3.152 亿美元。1986 年 10 月 23 日，里根又签署了美国众、参两院分别批准的修正税法，即 1986 年税制改革法案。这是战后最大规模的一次减税行动，根据这一法案，降低了个人所得税的最高税率，不同阶层的税率都有所下降，全国人均免税额减少了 6.4%，七年内每个家庭每年可支配收入约增加 600~900 美元。

放松政府对企业规章制度的限制，减少国家对企业的干预。20 世纪六七十年代，美政府对企业的管制活动达到了一个高峰。从一系列数据中可见："联邦登记册"中联邦管制条例从 1936 年的 2,599 页增加到 1977 年的 65,603 页，条例数量在 20 世纪 70 年代增加了 300%。在管制机构的从业人数从 1970 年的 2.8 万人增加到 1979 年的 8.1 万人。人们估计在 1980 年，单是执行当时美国已有的规章制度，每年就需要耗费 12 亿小时的工作量。如果每小时工作量的工资成本折合 20 美元，那么总开支超过 360 亿美元！同时，过多的政府干预妨碍了市场的自由发展，压制了企业的自主权和灵活性，扼杀了企业的创新力。里根上台不久就为管制改革制定了 10 项指导方针，这一系列措施对恢复市场经济活力起了很大的作用。

严格控制货币供应量的增长，实行稳定的货币政策。1979 年美国通用率高达 13.3%，而 20 世纪 60 年代初期的通用率还不到 2%，通货膨胀达到惊人地步。里根就任总统后在电视演说中亦承认，1960 年的 1 美元到 1981 年只值 36 美分，他上台后实行了严格紧缩货币政策，严控货币发行量，实行高利率。严控的效果十分明显，1980 年通货膨胀率为 18%，到 1987 年降到 3%。物价由 1980 年的 12.4% 下降到 1982 年的 3.9%。而高利率政策使 1985~1986 年每年有近 1,000 亿美元资金流入美国，刺激了美国经济的回升。

里根的一系列经济政策在 1982 年底开始初显成效，到 1983 年

二、三季度效果变得显著，1983 年 8 月，美国工业生产指数连续上升了九个月，已十分接近危机前的高点。当年 GDP 增长 4.5%，其中几个季度经济增长水平高达 8%。1983 年全年共增加 350 万个就业岗位，这一趋势延续到 1984 年美国总统大选年。当 1984 年里根谋求竞选连任时问选民："你们是不是比四年以前生活得更好？"美国人民回馈他的是四十八个州的压倒性胜利和高达 60% 的支持率。在他第二任期里美国经济进一步复苏，经济发展的强势令人瞩目，财政赤字减少了将近一半。

《福布斯》杂志曾评选出美国最会搞经济的总统是比尔·克林顿，因为克林顿时期联邦政府财政终于由赤字转为盈余，在其卸任时联邦政府预算盈余高达近 2,110 亿美元。但军功章上少不了里根的功劳，因为克林顿 1993 年接手的是冷战结束后通货膨胀率低，由技术推动发展的经济。里根政府使深陷滞胀泥潭的美国经济得以复苏，经济的调整，赤字的缩减，科技的大力发展以及唯一超级大国地位的确立和对世界市场的开拓，都为克林顿时期的经济辉煌打下了坚实、良好的基础。20 世纪 90 年代的辉煌离不开 20 世纪 80 年代的耕耘。

2005 年一档收集了美国历史上有较大影响力人物的电视节目热播，并最终由数百万名观众提名票选出他们心中"最伟大的美国人"，前十名的榜单上有林肯、马丁·路德·金、乔治·华盛顿、克林顿、富兰克林·罗斯福等影响美国深远的政界名人，而名列"最伟大的美国人"榜首的却是罗纳德·里根！盖洛普公司 2011 年民调时向受访者提问："你认为谁是美国最伟大的总统？"里根亦获得了最高票数。大器晚成的里根七十八岁离任时仍有着高达 63% 的支持率，里根曾这样自我评价："我们取得了两项胜利，两件让我感到自豪

的事情，一是经济实现了复苏，美国人民创造了 1,900 万个新的工作机会。另一个是美国人的道德精神得到了恢复。"他获得的赞誉不仅来自国内，亦是世界性的。20 世纪 80 年代，在撒切尔夫人和里根的领导下，一个老牌帝国，一个新晋超级大国，都成功地进行了经济变革。不管是撒切尔夫人医治"英国病"的"回春术"，还是里根经济学，都开拓了新的资本主义经济发展模式，这在资本主义国家乃至世界都有着广泛而积极的影响。

里根挽救了 20 世纪 80 年代美国经济的颓势，而他对世界的影响也是巨大的。他对世界最大的贡献是协助并加速了冷战的结束。在里根执政期间，美苏的军备竞赛达到了高峰，里根政府更不惜心血打造"星球大战计划"，但在他执政后期，与前苏联政府开始了"非常重要同时也是异常艰难的对话"，最终与戈尔巴乔夫达成共识，终止了军备竞赛，着手消除核武器，继而结束冷战。波兰团结工会的领导人列赫·瓦文萨说："我们所得到的自由是他给予的。"西德的总理赫尔穆特·科尔则说："他的出现是这个世界的幸运。在里根呼吁戈尔巴乔夫推倒柏林墙后的两年，柏林墙就真的倒了，而十一个月后德国便统一了。"后来成为捷克斯洛伐克总统的瓦茨拉夫·哈维尔说道："他是个抱持着坚定原则的人，毫无疑问是他促使了极权的垮台。"甚至曾身处敌对阵营的戈尔巴乔夫也评价道："他是个热爱生命的鹰派，他是个尊重常规价值的人。"

2004 年 6 月里根逝世后，他的忠实盟友兼好友英国前首相撒切尔夫人在悼词中总结了里根的功绩："其他人预言西方将走向衰落；他则激励美国及其盟国，继承实现自由使命的信念。……其他人惴惴不安地期待与苏联共存的最好结果；他却赢得了这场冷战——不仅一弹未发，而且邀请他的对手走出堡垒，化敌为友。"

里根最有效地演绎了美国的自由与民主精神，里根的经济学重新定位了国家与市场的关系，重组了美国的经济结构，而他最大的遗产是重拾了美国精神，恢复了大国的荣耀和信心，获得"完全的自由、尊严和机会"，他成为了美国人的榜样，也赢得了世界的喝彩。

第二节 里根于 1989 年在白宫发表告别演说

My fellow Americans:

This is the 34th time I'll speak to you from the Oval Office and the last. We've been together 8 years now, and soon it will be time for me to go. But before I do, I wanted to share some thoughts, some of which I have been saving for a long time.

It's been the honor of my life to be your President. So many of you have written the past few weeks to say thanks, but I could say as much to you. Nancy and I are grateful for the opportunity you gave us to serve.

One of the things about the Presidency is that you're always somewhat apart. You spent a lot of time going by too fast in a car someone else is driving, and seeing the people through tinted glass— the parents holding up a child, and the wave you saw too late and could not return. And so many times, I wanted to stop and reach out from behind the glass, and connect. Well, maybe I can do a little of that tonight.

People ask how I feel about leaving. And the fact is, "parting is such sweet sorrow." The sweet part is California and the ranch and freedom. The sorrow—the goodbyes, of course, and leaving this beautiful place.

You know, down the hall and up the stairs from this office is the part of the White House where the President and his family live. There are a few favorite windows I have up there that I like to stand and look out of early in the morning. The view is over the grounds here to the Washington Monument, and then the Mall and the Jefferson Memorial. But on mornings when the humidity is low, you can see past the Jefferson to the river, the Potomac, and the Virginia shore. Someone said that's the view Lincoln had when he saw the smoke rising from the Battle of Bull Run. Well I see more prosaic things: the grass on the banks, the morning traffic as people make their way to work, now and then a sailboat on the river.

I've been thinking a bit at that window. I've been reflecting on what the past 8 years have meant and mean. And the image that comes to mind like a refrain is a nautical one—a small story about a big ship, and a refugee, and a sailor.

It was back in the early eighties, at the height of the boat people. And the sailor was hard at work on the carrier Midway, which was patrolling the South China Sea. The sailor, like most American servicemen, was young, smart, and fiercely observant. The crew spied on the horizon a leaky little boat. And crammed inside were refugees from Indochina hoping to get to America. The Midway sent a small launch to bring them to the ship and safety. As the refugees made

their way through the choppy seas, one spied the sailor on deck, and stood up, and called out to him. He yelled, "Hello, American sailor. Hello, freedom man."

A small moment with a big meaning, a moment the sailor, who wrote it in a letter, couldn't get out of his mind. And, when I saw it, neither could I.

Because that's what it has to, it was to be an American in the 1980's. We stood, again, for freedom. I know we always have, but in the past few years the world again—and in a way, we ourselves— rediscovered it.

It's been quite a journey this decade, and we held together through some stormy seas. And at the end, together, we're reaching our destination.

The fact is, from Grenada to the Washington and Moscow summits, from the recession of '81 to '82, to the expansion that began in late '82 and continues to this day, we've made a difference.

The way I see it, there were two great triumphs, two things that I'm proudest of. One is the economic recovery, in which the people of America created—and filled—19 million new jobs. The other is the recovery of our morale. America is respected again in the world and looked to for leadership.

Something that happened to me a few years ago reflects some of this. It was back in 1981, and I was attending my first big economic summit, which was held that year in Canada. The meeting place rotates among the member countries. The opening meeting was a formal dinner for the heads of government of the seven industrialized nations. Well I sat there like the new kid in school and listened, and it was all Francois this and Helmut that. They dropped titles and spoke to one another on a first-name basis. Well, at one point I sort of leaned in and said, "My name's Ron."

Well, in that same year, we began the actions we felt would ignite an economic comeback—cut taxes and regulation, started to cut spending. And soon the recovery began.

Two years later, another economic summit with pretty much the same cast. At the big opening meeting we all got together, and all of a sudden, just for a moment, I saw that everyone was just sitting there looking at me. And then one of them broke the silence. "Tell us about the American miracle," he said.

Well, back in 1980, when I was running for President, it was all so different. Some pundits said our programs would result in catastrophe. Our views on foreign affairs would cause war. Our plans for the economy would cause inflation to soar and bring about economic collapse. I even remember one highly respected economist saying, back in 1982, that "The engines of economic growth have shut down here, and they're likely to stay that way for years to come."

Well, he and the other opinion leaders were wrong. The fact is what they call "radical" was really "right" . What they called "dangerous" was just "desperately needed" .

And in all of that time I won a nickname, "The Great Communicator." But I never thought it was my style or the words I used that made a difference: it was the content. I wasn't a great communicator, but I communicated great things, and they didn't spring full bloom from my brow, they came from the heart of a great

nation—from our experience, our wisdom, and our belief in the principles that have guided us for two centuries.

They called it the "Reagan Revolution." Well, I'll accept that, but for me it always seemed more like the great rediscovery, a rediscovery of our values and our common sense.

Common sense told us that when you put a big tax on something, the people would produce less of it. So, we cut the people's tax rates, and the people produced more than ever before. The economy bloomed like a plant that had been cut back and could now grow quicker and stronger. Our economic program brought about the longest peacetime expansion in our history: real family income up, the poverty rate down, entrepreneurship booming, and an explosion in research and new technology. We're exporting more than ever because American industry became more competitive. And at the same time, we summoned the national will to knock down protectionist walls abroad instead of erecting them at home.

Common sense also told us that to preserve the peace, we'd have to become strong again after years of weakness and confusion. So, we rebuilt our defenses, and this New Year we toasted the new peacefulness around the globe. Not only have the superpowers actually begun to reduce their stockpiles of nuclear weapons—and hope for even more progress is bright—but the regional conflicts that rack the globe are also beginning to cease. The Persian Gulf is no longer a war zone. The Soviets are leaving Afghanistan. The Vietnamese are preparing to pull out of Cambodia, and an American-mediated accord will soon send 50,000 Cuban troops home from Angola.

The lesson of all this was, of course, that because we're a great nation, our challenges seem complex. It will always be this way. But as long as we remember our first principles and believe in ourselves, the future will always be ours. And something else we learned: Once you begin a great movement, there's no telling where it'll end. We meant to change a nation, and instead, we changed a world.

Countries across the globe are turning to free markets and free speech and turning away from the ideologies of the past. For them, the great rediscovery of the 1980's has been that, lo and behold, the moral way of government is the practical way of government: Democracy, the profoundly good, is also the profoundly productive.

When you've got to the point when you can celebrate the anniversaries of your 39th birthday, you can sit back sometimes, review your life, and see it flowing before you. For me there was a fork in the river, and it was right in the middle of my life.

I never meant to go into politics. It wasn't my intention when I was young. But I was raised to believe you had to pay your way for the blessings bestowed on you. I was happy with my career in the entertainment world, but I ultimately went into politics because I wanted to protect something precious.

Ours was the first revolution in the history of mankind that truly reversed the course of government, and with three little words: "We the People." "We the People" tell the government what to do; it doesn't tell us. "We the People" are the driver; the government is the car, and we decide where it should go, and by what route, and how fast. Almost all the world's constitutions are documents in which governments tell the people what their privileges are. Our Constitution

is a document in which "We the People" tell the government what it is allowed to do. "We the People" are free. This belief has been the underlying basis for everything I've tried to do these past 8 years.

But back in the 1960's, when I began, it seemed to me that we'd begun reversing the order of things—that through more and more rules and regulations and confiscatory taxes, the government was taking more of our money, more of our options, and more of our freedom. I went into politics in part to put up my hand and say, "Stop." I was a citizen politician, and it seemed the right thing for a citizen to do.

I think we have stopped a lot of what needed stopping. And I hope we have once again reminded people that man is not free unless government is limited. There is a clear cause and effect here that is as neat and predictable as a law of physics: "As government expands, liberty contracts."

Nothing is less free than pure communism—and yet we have, the past few years, forged a satisfying new closeness with the Soviet Union. I've been asked if this isn't a gamble, and my answer is no because we're basing our actions not on words but deeds.

The detente of this 1970's was based not on actions but promises. They'd promise to treat their own people and the people of the world better. But the gulag was still the gulag, and the state was still expansionist, and they still waged proxy wars in Africa, Asia, and Latin America.

Well, this time, so far, it's different. President Gorbachev has brought about some internal democratic reforms and begun the withdrawal from Afghanistan. He has also freed prisoners whose names I've given him every time we've met.

But life has a way of reminding you of big things through small incidents. Once, during the heady days of the Moscow summit, Nancy and I decided to break off from the entourage one afternoon to visit the shops on Rabat Street—that's a little street just off Moscow's main shopping area. Even though our visit was a surprise, every Russian there immediately recognized us and called out our names and reached for our hands. We were just about swept away by the warmth. You could almost feel the possibilities in all that joy. But within seconds, a KGB detail pushed their way toward us and began pushing and shoving the people in the crowd. It was an interesting moment. It reminded me that while the man on the street in the Soviet Union yearns for peace, the government is Communist. And those who run it are Communists, and that means we and they view such issues as freedom and human rights very differently.

We must keep up our guard, but we must also continue to work together to lessen and eliminate tension and mistrust.

My view is that President Gorbachev is different from previous Soviet leaders. I think he knows some of the things wrong with his society and is trying to fix them. We wish him well. And we'll continue to work to make sure that the Soviet Union that eventually emerges from this process is a less threatening one. What it all boils down to is this: I want the new closeness to continue. And it will, as long as we make it clear that we will continue to act in a certain way as long as they continue to act in a helpful manner. If and when they don't, at first pull your punches. If they persist, pull the plug.

It is still trust but verify.

It is still play, but cut the cards.

It's still watch closely. And don't be afraid to see what you see.

I've been asked if I have any regrets. Well, I do. The deficit is one. I've been talking a great deal about that lately, but tonight isn't for arguments, and I'm going to hold my tongue.

But an observation: I've had my share of victories in the Congress, but what few people noticed is that I never won anything you didn't win for me. They never saw my troops; they never saw Reagan's regiments, the American people. You won every battle with every call you made and letter you wrote demanding action.

Well, action is still needed. If we're to finish the job, Reagan's regiments will have to become the Bush brigades. Soon he'll be the Chief, and he'll need you every bit as much as I did.

Finally, there is a great tradition of warnings in Presidential farewells, and I've got one that's been on my mind for some time.

But oddly enough it starts with one of the things I'm proudest of in the past 8 years: the resurgence of national pride that I called, "The New Patriotism." This national feeling is good, but it won't count for much, and it won't last unless it's grounded in thoughtfulness and knowledge.

An informed patriotism is what we want. And are we doing a good enough job teaching our children what America is and what she represents in the long history of the world?

Those of us who are over 35 or so years of age grew up in a different America. We were taught, very directly, what it means to be an American. And we absorbed, almost in the air, a love of country and an appreciation of its institutions. If you didn't get these things from your family you got them from the neighborhood, from the father down the street who fought in Korea or the family who lost someone at Anzio. Or you could get a sense of patriotism from school. And if all else failed you could get a sense of patriotism from the popular culture. The movies celebrated democratic values and implicitly reinforced the idea that America was special. TV was like that, too, through the mid-sixties.

But now, we're about to enter the nineties, and some things have changed. Younger parents aren't sure that an unambivalent appreciation of America is the right thing to teach modern children. And as for those who create the popular culture, well-grounded patriotism is no longer the style.

Our spirit is back, but we haven't reinstitutionalized it. We've got to do a better job of getting across that America is freedom—freedom of speech, freedom of religion, freedom of enterprise. And freedom is special and rare. It's fragile; it needs production.

So, we've got to teach history based not on what's in fashion but what's important—why the Pilgrims came here, who Jimmy Doolittle was, and what those 30 seconds over Tokyo meant. You know, 4 years ago on the 40th anniversary of D-day, I read a letter from a young woman writing to her late father, who had fought on Omaha Beach. Her name was Lisa Zanatta Henn, and she said, "we will always remember, we will never forget what the boys of Normandy did." Well, let us help her keep her word. If we forget what we did, we won't know who we are. I'm warning of an eradication of that—of the American memory that could result, ultimately, in an erosion of the American spirit. Let us start with some basics: more attention to

American history and a greater emphasis on civic ritual.

And let me offer lesson number one about America: All great change in America begins at the dinner table. So, tomorrow night in the kitchen I hope the talking begins. And children, if your parents haven't been teaching you what it means to be an American, let's know and nail on it. That would be a very American thing to do.

And that's about all I have to say tonight, except for one thing.

The past few days when I've been at that window upstairs, I've thought a bit of the shining city upon a hill. The phrase comes from John Winthrop, who wrote it to describe the America he imagined. What he imagined was important because he was an early Pilgrim, an early freedom man. He journeyed here on what today we'd call a little wooden boat; and like the other Pilgrims, he was looking for a home that would be free.

I've spoken of the shining city all my political life, but I don't know if I ever quite communicated what I saw when I said it. But in my mind it was a tall, proud city built on rocks stronger than oceans, windswept, God-blessed, and teeming with people of all kinds living in harmony and peace; a city with free ports that hummed with commerce and creativity. And if there had to be city walls, the walls had doors and the doors were open to anyone with the will and the heart to get here. That's how I saw it, and see it still.

And how stands the city on this winter night? More prosperous, more secure, and happier than it was 8 years ago. But more than that: After 200 years, two centuries, she still stands strong and true on the granite ridge, and her glow has held steady no matter what storm. And she's still a beacon, still a magnet for all who must have freedom, for all the pilgrims from all the lost places who are hurtling through the darkness, toward home.

We've done our part. And as I walk off into the city streets, a final word to the men and women of the Reagan Revolution, the men and women across America who for 8 years did the work that brought America back.

My friends: We did it. We weren't just marking time. We made a difference. We made the city stronger; we made the city freer; and we left her in good hands.

All in all, not bad—not bad at all.

And so, goodbye, God bless you, and God bless the United States of America.

同胞们：

这是我第三十四次，也是最后一次在椭圆形办公室向你们讲话。我们在一起共事至今已有八年，而此时我卸任的时刻即将到来。但是，在此之前，我愿与你们共享我的心得，其中一些我已深思许久了。

成为你们的总统是我终身的光荣。过去几周，许多人来信表示谢意，但是，我更要向你们说声谢谢。南希和我感谢你们给了我们为美国效力的机会。

作为一名总统，一个特殊之处就在于我总是多少有点与世隔绝之感。我花费许多宝贵的时间乘坐在一辆由别人驾驶的轿车里，透过染色玻璃注视着人们——抱着孩子的父母，以及窗外一晃而过的人流。多少次我想让司机停车，从车窗后面伸出手来与人们打招呼并作一番交流，或许今晚我能够实现这一心愿。

有人问我离去的感受，离去当然是"如此甜蜜而又令人伤感"。甜蜜是因为就要回到加利福尼亚，在牧场上漫步，享受自由的时光。那么何谓伤感呢？当然是离别，是离开这美丽的地方。

如你们所知，走下大厅，再从这间办公室走上楼梯，就是白宫中供总统及其家人居住的地方。楼上有几扇精美的窗子。我喜欢在黎明时分伫立着眺望窗外的景色。从这里眺望过去，是华盛顿纪念碑，然后是林荫大道，杰斐逊纪念堂。在晴朗的早晨，越过杰斐逊纪念堂，你能够看到一条河流——波托马克河和弗吉尼亚海滨。人们传说，这就是当年林肯在注视从布尔伦河战场上腾起的烟雾时所见到的景色。我见到的景色更为平淡：河岸上的草地，早晨上班途中的车辆和行人，以及河面上偶尔飘过的一叶帆船。

我时常在那扇窗户旁苦苦思考。我时常反思过去的八年和现在究竟意味着什么。进入脑海的是一幅被一再描绘的画面——一个关于一艘船、一个难民和一位水兵的故事。

回顾20世纪80年代初，当时，从印度支那乘船出逃的难民正达到高潮，而在南中国海巡航的中途岛号航母上，这名水兵正在勤劳地干着活。这名水兵像大多数美国军人一样，年轻、聪明、敏锐。水兵们发现，在遥远的地平线上有一艘小船正在波涛中沉浮——船上挤满了渴望去美国的印支难民。于是，中途岛号派出一艘小型汽艇去接应他们。难民们在波涛汹涌的大海中挣扎，其中的一位难民发现了甲板上的那位水兵，便站起身来，向他呼喊道："你好，美国水兵，你好，自由人。"

一个毫不起眼但又意义重大的时刻，一个令人难以忘怀的时刻——这名水兵在一封信中这样写道。假如我也曾目睹这一时刻，那么我也将无法忘怀。

因为这就是 20 世纪 80 年代，作为一名美国人所具有的含义。我们再一次象征着自由。我深信我们一直代表着自由，但是在过去数年间，世界再次——在某种程度上我们自己——也重新发现了这一点。

十年来，这确实是一次艰难的旅程，我们同舟共济，穿越了狂风暴雨的大海。最终，我们一起到达了理想的彼岸。

事实上，从梅林纳达到华盛顿和莫斯科峰会，从 1981 至 1982 年的经济衰退，到始于 1982 年年末，并一直持续至今的经济增长，我们已经创造了奇迹。

依我看来，我们取得了两项我为此而感到无比自豪的巨大成就。一项是经济的复苏，美国人民创造并且胜任了 1,900 万个新的工作岗位。另一项是道德的恢复，美国再次受到世界的尊重，并被寄予厚望来承担起领导世界的重任。

几年前，我亲身经历的某些事情多少反映了这种变化。回想 1981 年，我首次出席在加拿大召开的一次大型经济问题峰会。会议地点在各成员国中轮流。公开会议是为西方七国政府首脑举行的一次宴会。我就像学校里的一名新生，坐在一旁倾听，满耳不是弗兰科斯就是赫尔穆特。大家彼此之间不称职衔，而是直呼其名以示亲密。当时，我几乎是俯下身来说道："我叫罗纳德"。

同年，我开始采取我们认为可能导致经济复苏的一些措施：减少税收、放松控制、削减支出。不久，经济开始复苏。

两年后，又一届经济问题峰会召开，与会者与上届极为相似。在大型公开会议上，我们汇聚在一起。忽然，我出乎意料地发现他们都注视着我。接着，其中的一位打破沉默说道："给我们谈谈美国发生的奇迹。"

回想 1980 年，当我竞选总统时，情况却与此大相径庭。一些权威人士说，我们的计划将导致灾难。我们的外交观点将引发战争，我们的经济计划将引起恶性通胀，导致经济崩溃。我对一位备受尊敬的经济学家在 1982 年所说的话还记忆犹新，他说："在美国，在全世界，带动经济增长的火车头已经停顿下来，并且在未来的数年里可能毫无起色。"

然而，他以及其他舆论界的领袖们都错了。事实上，他们称之为"激进的"无疑是"正确的"，他们称之为"危险的"恰恰是"急需的"。

总之，那时我赢得了一个绰号"伟大的传播者"。但是，我从不认为这是我的风格，或者我使用的语言改造了世界，这是问题的关键，我不是一位伟大的传播者，但是我传播了伟大的思想，它们并非凭空出自我的头脑，它们来自一个伟大的国家的内心——来自我们的经历、我们的智慧以及我们对两个世纪里引导我们的那些原则的信念。

他们将它称之为里根革命，我接受这种说法。但是就我而言，这似乎更像是伟大的再发现：我们的价值观念与一致公认的常识的一次再发现。

常识告诉我们，当你必须为某件商品交纳大笔税款时，人们就会减少生产这种商品。因此，我们削减了国民的税率，而国民却生产得比以往更多。我国的经济就像一棵被修剪过的大树，现在生长得更加迅速，更加根深叶茂了。我们的经济计划促成了我国历史上，在和平年代最长的一次经济增长：家庭纯收入提高了、贫困率下降了、工商界兴旺发达、科研和新技术迅猛发展。我们比以往任何时候都出口更多，因为美国的企业变得更具竞争力。同时，我们确立了这样一种国家意志：我们与其在国内构筑保护主义壁垒，不如去拆除国外的保护主义壁垒。

常识还告诉我们，为了维护和平，我们必须在经历数年的软弱和混乱之后再次变得强大。因此，我们重建了我们的防务——值此新年来临之际，我们为全球的和平而举杯。事实上，超级大国不仅已开始削减核武器储备，甚至取得更大的进展的前景同样是明朗的，而且令世界备感不安的地区冲突也即将结束。波斯湾不再是交战地区，苏联正在从阿富汗撤离，越南即将撤出柬埔寨，而经美国斡旋签署的一项协议，不久将使五万名古巴军人离开安哥拉回国。

当然，从所有这些事件中得出的教训是，由于我们是一个伟大的国家，因此我们面临的挑战是错综复杂的，并且将永远如此。但是，只要我们牢记我们的基本原则，并且相信自己，那么未来永远是我们的。我们还懂得了，一旦你开始采取某项行动，那么就难以预料将何时结束。我们只是要改变一个国家，却改变了整个世界。

世界各国正在向自由市场转型，开始允许言论自由，抛弃过去的意识形态。对它们而言，20 世纪 80 年代的大发现，我们是道德的政府也是富有成效的政府，民主不仅是极其美好的，也是极具经济价值的。

在你们庆祝三十九岁生日的时候，你们能够休息片刻，回顾一下你们的人生，注视着时光在你们的面前流逝。对于我来说，则犹如河中的树枝，正漂流至我生命旅程的中途。

我从未想过步入政坛，这也不是我年轻时的志向。但是我从小就接受这样的教诲，相信你自己必须为你所得到的恩赐付出代价。我对从事演艺业感到满意，但是我最终进入政界，是因为我要保护一些弥足珍贵的东西。

我们所经历的变革，是人类历史上"我们的人民"真正改变了政府的演变进程的第一次革命。"我们的人民"告诉政府，而不是政府告诉"我们的人民"该做什么。"我们的人民"是驾驶员，而政府则是一辆汽车。"我们的人民"决定它行驶的方向、道路与速度。世界上几乎所有国家的宪法都是告诉人民享有哪些特权。而在我们的宪法告诉政府应该怎样做，"我们的人民"是自由的。这种信念是我在过去八年里作出不懈努力的基础。

但是，回想20世纪60年代，当我开始投身政治时，我们似乎把一切都颠倒了——政府通过越来越多的法规和赋税条例，正在更多地剥夺我们的钱财、我们的选择权以及我们的自由。我之所以步入政坛，在某种程度上，就是要举起我的手，大喝一声："住手！"我是一名平民政治家，这是一个平民应尽的责任。

我认为我们阻止了大量本该阻止的事情的发生或延续。我们再次提醒了人们，除非政府的权力受到限制，否则人类是不会自由的。两者之间的因果关系如同物理定律一样简单明了。可以预料，政府膨胀一分，则自由收缩一分。

没有比纯粹的极权主义更不自由的，然而，在过去几年，我们已同苏联建立了新型的令人满意的密切联系。我曾经扪心自间，这难道不是一种赌博吗？我的回答是否定的。因为我们的决断是建立在行动上，而不是建立在言辞上的。

20世纪70年代缓和的基础，不是行动而是许诺。他们许诺善待他们本国和世界各国的人民，但是古拉格还是古拉格，苏联依然是扩张主义国家，他们依然在非洲、亚洲和拉丁美训进行傀儡战争。

现在的情况已有所不同，戈尔巴乔夫在国内已着手进行某些民主改革，并已开始撤离阿富汗。他还释放了我们每次会晤时，我向他提供了姓名的那些犯人。

但是，生活能够通过一些细节使你们回想起某些重要的事情。在莫斯科峰会期间那些令人兴奋的日子里，一天上午，南希和我决定摆脱随行人员，独自去莫斯科主要购物区近旁的一条街——阿尔巴特大街上的商店去逛逛。尽管我们的到访出乎人们的意料，但是那里的每一个俄罗斯人都立刻认出了我们，呼喊我们的名字，与我们握手。我们几乎被这种热情所吞没，假如你们身临其境，那么你们可能也会有这种感觉。但是片刻之后，一队克格勃奋力朝我们挤来，并且开始推搡人群。这是一个多么有趣的时刻，它提醒我当苏联大街上的人们渴望和平的时候，而该国的政府却是极权主义的。这意味着在诸如自由和人权等问题上，我们与他们的观点是截然不同的。

我们必须保持警惕，但是我们同样必须继续保持合作，减少并且消除紧张和不信任。

我认为戈尔巴乔夫总统与以前的苏联领导人不同。我认为他了解苏联社会中存在的那些弊病，并且正在试图加以解决。我们预祝他成功。他们将继续努力，以确保在经历这一进程以后而获得新生的苏联，将不再是一个咄咄逼人的国家。归结起来就是我希望继续保持这种新型的密切关系。如同我们表明的那样，我们将始终视他们是否以一种有益的方式行事，来决定我们将采取何种行动。如果一旦他们并非如此，那么首先好言相劝，如果他们执迷不悟，那么不妨动真格的。

我们之间仍然是互相信任的，但需要得到证实。

游戏还得玩下去，但必须重新开始。

我们还要密切关注事态的发展，并且不惧怕面对所目睹的一切。

曾经有人问我，是否有遗憾之处。有的。如赤字就是其中之一。近来，我对此问题谈了许多，但是今晚不宜再作讨论，我愿保持缄默。

有人认为我分享了国会的胜利成果，然而几乎无人意识到，我的胜利无不是由你们创造的。他们从不正视我的部队，从不正视里根团，即美国人民。你们发出召唤，发布文告以动员人民，赢得了每一次战斗。

行动仍然是必不可少的。如果我们想要完成这项工作，那么里根团就应当成为布什旅。不久他将成为一个领袖，他像我一样需要你们。

最后我要说的是，总统告别演说具有向人们提出忠告这样一个伟大的传统，而我确有一个忠告，它在我的脑海里已酝酿许久。

但是，说来奇怪，它是以我在过去八年里引以为豪的事物之一，即被我称作为"新爱国主义"的民族自豪感的再次振兴作为开场白的。这种民族自豪感无可非议，但其价值并非很高，并且不会持久，除非这种情感是建立在思考和知识的基础上的。

我们需要的是明智的爱国主义。那么，我们是否出色地教育了我们的孩子，使其懂得美国意味着什么？在漫长的世界史上，它又代表着什么？

我们年过三十五岁的那些人，生长在一个与今不同的美国。我们被直截了当地告之，做一个美国人意味着什么？我们几乎能够在吸入的空气中感受到对国家的热爱以及对制度的赏识。假如你无法从你的家人那里感受到这种爱和这种赏识，那么你仍然能够从邻居那里，从在韩国进行街头斗争的前辈那里，或者从在安齐奥失去亲人的那些家庭那里感受到。假如你还感受不到，那么你依然能够从大众文化那里感受到爱国主义意识。电影赞颂了民主的价值，并且潜移默化地增强了美国是无与伦比的这种观念。在整个 20 世纪 60 年代中期，电视同样如此。

但是，现在我们即将进入 20 世纪 90 年代，有些情况已发生了变化。年轻的父母们无法确信，对美国不加掩饰的赏识，是否仍然是教育现代孩子们的灵丹妙药。至于对那些创造大众文化的人们来说，具有真凭实据的爱国主义已不再是一种时尚。

我们的精神已经过时，但是我们尚未重建一种精神。我们必须加倍努力，以使人们相信美国象征着自由——言论自由、宗教自由、经营自由。而自由是独特而又富有价值的。它是脆弱的，需要得到保护。

我们应当不是基于考虑是否符合时尚，而是考虑是否重要来教授早期移民为何来到这里的历史，吉米·杜立德是谁，那 30 秒对东京意味着什么？你们是否知道，四年前在诺曼底登陆四十周年纪念日，我读到一封一位女青年写给曾参加过奥马哈海滩之战的已故父亲的信。她叫莉萨·詹纳特·亨，她写道："我们永远铭记，我们终身不忘参加诺曼底之战的小伙子们的伟业。"让我们助她以一臂之力，以恪守这一诺言吧！假如我们忘掉了历史，那么也就意味着忘掉了自己。在此，我对美国人的健忘发出警告，这种健忘将导致美国精神的堕落。让我们从一些基本的事情做起：更加关注美国的历史，更加重视公民的礼仪。

请让我提出与美国有关的最重要的一条教训：美国所有重大的变革都是从餐桌上开始的。因此，我希望明晚在厨房里开始谈话。孩子们，如果你们的父母从未告诉过你们，当一个美国人意味着什么——那么让他们知道并且记住，这是任何一位真正的美国人都不容推辞的责任。

这就是今晚我要说的全部内容。另外，还要补充一点。

最近几天，当我伫立在楼上的窗边时，对这座"屹立在山岗上的"辉煌的城市想了许多。这一说法源自约翰·温思罗普，他以此来描述他想象中的美国。他的想象十分重要，因为他是一位早期移民——一位早期的"自由人"。他乘坐我们现在称之为小木船的那种船来到这里，并且像其他早期移民一样，他渴望拥有一个自由的家园。

在我的整个政治生涯中，我曾经一再地谈起这座辉煌的城市，但是，我不知道是否清楚地表达了我的思想。在我的心目中，这是一座高大得令人骄傲的城市，它建立在坚实的基石上，而绝非是一座空中楼阁。上帝保佑着她，街上人来人往，各种肤色的人们生活在和睦与和平之中。一座拥有自由港、商业繁荣并且具有创造性的城市。如果这座城市建有城墙，那么一定是有城门的，并且是向所有梦寐以求要来到这里的人们敞开的。这曾经是并且依然是我的看法。

在这寒冷的冬夜，这座城市又会如何呢？它比八年前更加繁荣、更加安全、更加幸福了。但不仅于此：两百年后，甚至两个世纪以后，它将更加强大，稳稳地屹立在花岗岩的山脊上，面对风暴依然熠熠发光。她将成为一座灯塔，或一块磁石，为所有一心向往自由的人们，为所有来自迷失之地，逃离黑暗回家的朝圣者们引路指航。

我们履行了自己的职责。当我走出这里来到这座城市的大街上时，我要向参与这场里根革命的男人和女人们——在过去八年里为复兴美国而工作的全国各地的男人和女人们道别。

朋友们，我们成功了。我们不仅追回了失去的时光，而且改变了世界。我们使这座城市变得更加坚固，更加自由，并且将她交给优秀者手中。

总之，情况不错，一切顺利。

再见了。上帝保佑你们。上帝保佑美利坚合众国。

第三节 精彩语录

I wasn't a great communicator, but I communicated great things, and they didn't spring full bloom from my brow, they came from the heart of a great nation—from our experience, our wisdom, and our belief in the principles that have guided us for two centuries.

我不是一位伟大的传播者，但是我传播了伟大的思想，它们并非凭空出自我的头脑，它们来自一个伟大的国家的内心——来自我们的经历、我们的智慧以及我们对两个世纪里引导我们的那些原则的信念。

Because we're a great nation, our challenges seem complex. It will always be this way. But as long as we remember our first principles and believe in ourselves, the future will always be ours.

由于我们是一个伟大的国家，因此我们面临的挑战是错综复杂的，并且将永远如此。但是，只要我们牢记我们的基本原则，并且相信自己，那么未来永远是我们的。

"We the People" tell the government what to do; it doesn't tell us. "We the People" are the driver; the government is the car, and we decide where it should go, and by what route, and how fast. Almost all the world's constitutions are documents in which governments tell the people what their privileges are. Our Constitution is a document in which"We the People"tell the government what it is allowed to do. "We the People" are free.

"我们的人民"告诉政府,而不是政府告诉"我们的人民"该做什么。"我们的人民"是驾驶员,而政府则是一辆汽车。"我们的人民"决定它行驶的方向、道路与速度。世界上几乎所有国家的宪法都是告诉人民享有哪些特权。而在我们的宪法告诉政府应该怎样做,"我们的人民"是自由的。

Our spirit is back, but we haven't reinstitutionalized it. We've got to do a better job of getting across that America is freedom—freedom of speech, freedom of religion, freedom of enterprise. And freedom is special and rare. It's fragile; it needs production.

我们的精神已经过时,但是我们尚未重建一种精神。我们必须加倍努力,以使人们相信美国象征着自由——言论自由、宗教自由、经营自由。而自由是独特而又富有价值的。它是脆弱的,需要得到保护。

第八章

以你的荣耀谱写天空的绚丽

第一节 背景介绍

　　参加诺曼底登陆战役，先后有 36 个师，总兵力达 288 万人，其中陆军有 153 万人，相当于 20 世纪末美国的全部军队。美英军队通过这次登陆重返欧洲大陆，使第二次世界大战的战略态势发生了根本性变化。这是目前为止世界上最大的一次海上登陆作战，也是战争史上最有影响的登陆战役之一。

　　战役发生在 1944 年 6 月 6 日晨 6 时 30 分。这次作战行动的代号为"霸王行动"。这场战役在 8 月 19 日盟军渡过塞纳·马恩省河后结束。从 1944 年 6 月 6 日至 7 月初，美国、英国、加拿大的百万军队，17 万辆军车，60 万吨各类补给品，成功地渡过了英吉利海峡。到 7 月 24 日，战争双方约有 24 万人被歼灭，其中盟军伤亡 12.2 万人，德军伤亡和被俘 11.4 万人。至 8 月底，盟军一共消灭或重创德军 40 个师，德军的三名元帅和一名集团军司令先后被撤职或离职，击毙和俘虏德军集团军司令、军长、师长等高级将领 20 人。德军损失飞机 3,500 架，坦克 1.3 万辆，各种车辆 2 万辆，人员 40 万。

早在 1941 年 9 月，斯大林就向丘吉尔提出在欧洲开辟第二战场，对德国实施战略夹击的要求，但当时美国尚未参战，英国根本无力组织这样大规模的战略登陆作战。对于苏联的建议，英国的回应只是派出小部队对欧洲大陆实施偷袭骚扰。

1942 年 6 月，苏美和苏英发表联合公报，达成在欧洲开辟第二战场的充分谅解和共识，但英国在备忘录中对承担的义务作了一些保留。

1942 年 7 月，英美伦敦会议决定 1942 年秋在北非登陆，而把在欧洲开辟第二战场推迟到 1943 年上半年。但此时苏德战场形势非常严峻，德军已进至斯大林格勒，苏联强烈要求英美在欧洲发动登陆作战，以牵制德军减轻苏军压力。英国只好仓促派出由 6,018 人组成的突击部队在法国第厄普登陆，结果遭到惨败，伤亡 5,810 人，伤亡率高达 96.5%。

1943 年 1 月，英美卡萨布兰卡会议，通过上半年在西西里岛登陆的决定。把在欧洲大陆的登陆推迟到 1943 年 8 月。在这次会议上，英国借第厄普的失败，以人规模两栖登陆的复杂与危险必须谨慎从事为理由，坚持要求推迟对欧洲大陆的登陆。实际上英国一则想乘苏德相争坐收渔翁之利，二则想借美国的力量恢复大英帝国战前在北非和南欧的传统势力。但遭到美国的反对，作为妥协英国同意成立英美特别计划参谋部，负责制订在欧洲的登陆计划。由英国陆军中将 F. 摩根担任参谋长。摩根上任后立即组建"考萨克"，"考萨克"就是同盟国欧洲远征军最高参谋部的英文缩写，主要成员有副参谋长美国陆军准将雷·巴克，陆、海、空军及所有与登陆有关的各军兵种代表，负责指挥对欧洲大陆偷袭骚扰作战的英国联

合作战司令部司令蒙巴顿海军中将当然也是其成员。

1943年5月，英美华盛顿会议决定于1944年5月在欧洲大陆实施登陆，开辟第二战场。"考萨克"立即开始制定登陆计划，首先确定登陆地点，根据历次登陆作战的经验教训，登陆地点要具备三个条件。一要在从英国机场起飞的战斗机半径内，二航渡距离要尽可能短，三附近要有大港口。那么从荷兰符利辛根到法国瑟堡长达480公里的海岸线上，以此条件衡量，有三处地区较为合适：康坦丁半岛、加莱和诺曼底。再进一步比较，康坦丁半岛地形狭窄，不便于展开大部队，最先被否决。加莱和诺曼底各有利弊，加莱的优点是距英国最近仅33公里，而且靠近德国本土；缺点是德军在此防御力量最强，守军是精锐部队，工事完备坚固，并且附近无大港口，也缺乏内陆交通线，不利于登陆后向纵深发展。诺曼底虽然距离英国较远，但优点一是德军防御较弱，二是地形开阔，可同时展开30个师，三是距法国北部最大港口瑟堡仅80公里。几经权衡比较，"考萨克"选择了诺曼底，于1943年6月26日起制定具体计划，以"霸王"为作战方案的代号，以"海王"为相关海军行动的代号。初步计划以3个师在卡朗坦至卡昂之间32公里宽的二个滩头登陆，即后来的"奥马哈""金"和"朱诺"滩头，同时空降2个旅。第二梯队为8个师，将在两周内占领瑟堡。整个计划中最大的难题是港口问题，也就是在占领瑟堡前，如何解决部队的后勤补给，要知道诺曼底在五六月间多为大风大浪，光靠登陆滩头无法保证后勤供应——这似乎成为无法克服的困难。束手无策中，"考萨克"的海军代表英国海军少将约翰·休斯·哈莱特想起蒙巴顿在一次会议上的玩笑：既然没有天然港口，就造一个人工港。于是建议制造配件装配成人工港来解决问题，别无良策他的设想获得批准。7月15日，摩根将"霸王"计划大纲呈交英美联合参谋长委员会。

1943 年 12 月，美国陆军上将艾森豪威尔被任命为欧洲同盟国远征军最高司令，于 1944 年 1 月 2 日抵达伦敦就任。艾森豪威尔阅读了摩根计划，认为突击正面太窄，在最初攻击中缺乏足够的突击力量，提出修改意见，把登陆正面扩大到 80 公里，第一梯队由 3 个师增加到 5 个师，登陆滩头也从 3 个增加到 5 个，空降兵从 2 个旅增加到 3 个师，这一意见得到最高司令部三军司令的支持。

1944 年 2 月，英美联合参谋长委员会批准了"霸王"计划大纲和修改后的作战计划，但是随之对登陆舰艇的需求也增加了，为了确保拥有足够的登陆舰艇，英美联合参谋长委员会决定将登陆日期推迟到 6 月初，并且将原定同时在法国南部的登陆推迟到 8 月。

由于登陆日推迟到 6 月初，盟军统帅部开始确定具体的日期和时刻，这是一个复杂的协同问题，各军兵种根据自己的需要提出不同要求。陆军要求在高潮上陆，以减少部队暴露在海滩上的时间；海军要求在低潮时上陆，以便尽量减少登陆艇遭到障碍物的破坏；空军要求有月光，便于空降部队识别地面目标。最后经认真考虑，拟定符合各军种的科学方案。在高潮与低潮间登陆，由于五个滩头的潮汐不尽相同，所以规定五个不同的登陆时刻，登陆日则安排在满月的日子，空降时间为凌晨 1 时 .符合上述条件的登陆日期，在 1944 年 6 月中只有两组连续三天的日子，6 月 5 日至 7 日，6 月 18 日至 20 日，最后选用第一组的第一天，即 6 月 5 日。

战役目的是横渡英吉利海峡，在法国北部夺取一个战略性登陆场，为开辟欧洲第二战场最终击败德国创造条件。战役计划在诺曼底登陆，夺取登陆场。在登陆的第 12 天，把登陆场扩展到宽 100 公里，纵深 100 公里。在登陆场右翼空降 2 个美国伞兵师，切断德

军从瑟堡出发的增援，并协同登陆部队夺取"犹他"滩头，在左翼空降 1 个英国伞兵师，夺取康恩运河的渡河点，然后首批 8 个加强营在 5 个滩头登陆，建立登陆场，在巩固和扩大登陆场后，后续部队上岸，右翼先攻占瑟堡，左翼向康恩河至圣罗一线发展，掩护右翼部队的攻击。第二阶段攻占冈城、贝叶、伊济尼、卡朗坦。第三阶段攻占布勒塔尼，向塞纳河推进，直取巴黎。

1944 年 1 月 21 日，艾森豪威尔就在诺福克旅馆召开了远征军最高司令部首次会议，在会议上明确了登陆作战的纲领，使这次会议成为二战中最重要的盟军军事会议。

进攻诺曼底在登陆的前一天晚上展开，空降兵空降作战，大规模的空中轰炸。而两栖登陆战则在 1944 年 6 月 6 日早上开始。在登陆前，"D-Day"的军队主要部署在英格兰南部沿海地区，尤其在朴茨茅斯。诺曼底战役持续了两个多月，最终，盟军成功建立滩头堡，并在 1944 年 8 月 25 日解放巴黎，宣告结束诺曼底战役。

诺曼底登陆战役是世界历史上规模最大的两栖登陆战役，是战略性的战役，为开辟欧洲的第二战场奠定了基础，对加速法西斯德国的崩溃以及战后欧洲局势，都起到了重要作用。

第二节 里根于 1984 年纪念诺曼底登陆四十周年演讲

We're here to mark that day in history when the Allied armies joined in battle to reclaim this continent to liberty.

For four long years, much of Europe had been under a terrible shadow. Free nations had fallen, Jews cried out in the camps, millions cried out for liberation. Europe was enslaved and the world prayed for its rescue. Here, in Normandy, the rescue began. Here, the Allies stood and fought against tyranny, in a giant undertaking unparalleled in human history.

We stand on a lonely, windswept point on the northern shore of France. The air is soft, but forty years ago at this moment, the air was dense with smoke and the cries of men, and the air was filled with the crack of rifle fire and the roar of cannon. At dawn, on the morning of the 6th of June, 1944, two hundred and twenty-five Rangers jumped off the British landing craft and ran to the bottom of these cliffs.

Their mission was one of the most difficult and daring of the

invasion: to climb these sheer and desolate cliffs and take out the enemy guns. The Allies had been told that some of the mightiest of these guns were here, and they would be trained on the beaches to stop the Allied advance.

The Rangers looked up and saw the enemy soldiers at the edge of the cliffs, shooting down at them with machine guns and throwing grenades. And the American Rangers began to climb. They shot rope ladders over the face of these cliffs and began to pull themselves up. When one Ranger fell, another would take his place. When one rope was cut, a Ranger would grab another and begin his climb again. They climbed, shot back, and held their footing. Soon, one by one, the Rangers pulled themselves over the top, and in seizing the firm land at the top of these cliffs, they began to seize back the continent of Europe. Two hundred and twenty-five came here. After two days of fighting, only ninety could still bear arms.

And behind me is a memorial that symbolizes the Ranger daggers that were thrust into the top of these cliffs. And before me are the men who put them there. These are the boys of Pointe du Hoc. These are the men who took the cliffs. These are the champions who helped free a continent. And these are the heroes who helped end a war. Gentlemen, I look at you and I think of the words of Stephen Spender's poem. You are men who in your "lives fought for life and left the vivid air signed with your honor."

I think I know what you may be thinking right now—thinking "we were just part of a bigger effort; everyone was brave that day." Well everyone was. Do you remember the story of Bill Millin of the 51st Highlanders? Forty years ago, today, British troops were pinned down near a bridge, waiting desperately for help. Suddenly, they heard the sound of bagpipes, and some thought they were dreaming. Well, they weren't. They looked up and saw Bill Millin with his bagpipes, leading the reinforcements and ignoring the smack of the bullets into the ground around him.

Lord Lovat was with him—Lord Lovat of Scotland, who calmly announced when he got to the bridge, "Sorry, I'm a few minutes late," as if he'd been delayed by a traffic jam, when in truth he'd just come from the bloody fighting on Sword Beach, which he and his men had just taken.

There was the impossible valor of the Poles, who threw themselves between the enemy and the rest of Europe as the invasion took hold; and the unsurpassed courage of the Canadians who had already seen the horrors of war on this coast. They knew what awaited them there, but they would not be deterred. And once they hit Juno Beach, they never looked back.

All of these men were part of a roll call of honor with names that spoke of a pride as bright as the colors they bore; The Royal Winnipeg Rifles, Poland's 24th Lancers, the Royal Scots' Fusiliers, the Screaming Eagles, the Yeomen of England's armored divisions, the forces of Free France, the Coast Guard's "Matchbox Fleet," and you, the American Rangers.

Forty summers have passed since the battle that you fought here. You were young the day you took these cliffs; some of you were hardly more than boys, with the deepest joys of life before you. Yet you risked everything here. Why? Why did you do it? What impelled you to put aside the instinct for self-preservation and risk your lives to take these

cliffs? What inspired all the men of the armies that met here? We look at you, and somehow we know the answer. It was faith and belief. It was loyalty and love.

The men of Normandy had faith that what they were doing was right, faith that they fought for all humanity, faith that a just God would grant them mercy on this beachhead, or on the next. It was the deep knowledge—and prays God we have not lost it—that there is a profound moral difference between the use of force for liberation and the use of force for conquest. You were here to liberate, not to conquer, and so you and those others did not doubt your cause. And you were right not to doubt.

You all knew that some things are worth dying for. One's country is worth dying for, and democracy is worth dying for, because it's the most deeply honorable form of government ever devised by man. All of you loved liberty. All of you were willing to fight tyranny, and you knew the people of your countries were behind you.

The Americans who fought here that morning knew word of the invasion was spreading through the darkness back home. They fought—or felt in their hearts, though they couldn't know in fact, that in Georgia they were filling the churches at 4:00 am. In Kansas they were kneeling on their porches and praying. And in Philadelphia they were ringing the Liberty Bell.

Something else helped the men of D-day; their rock-hard belief that Providence would have a great hand in the events that would unfold here; that God was an ally in this great cause. And so, the night before the invasion, when Colonel Walkerton asked his parachute troops to kneel with him in prayer, he told them: "Do not bow your heads, but look up so you can see God and ask His blessing in what we're about to do." Also, that night, General Matthew Ridgway on his cot, listening in the darkness for the promise God made to Joshua: "I will not fail thee nor forsake thee."

These are the things that impelled them; these are the things that shaped the unity of the Allies.

When the war was over, there were lives to be rebuilt and governments to be returned to the people. There were nations to be reborn. Above all, there was a new peace to be assured. These were huge and daunting tasks. But the Allies summoned strength from the faith, belief, loyalty, and love of those who fell here. They rebuilt a new Europe together. There was first a great reconciliation among those who had been enemies, all of whom had suffered so greatly. The United States did its part, creating the Marshall Plan to help rebuild our allies and our former enemies. The Marshall Plan led to the Atlantic alliance—a great alliance that serves to this day as our shield for freedom, for prosperity, and for peace.

In spite of our great efforts and successes, not all that followed the end of the war was happy or planned. Some liberated countries were lost. The great sadness of this loss echoes down to our own time in the streets of Warsaw, Prague, and East Berlin. The Soviet troops that came to the center of this continent did not leave when peace came. They're still there, uninvited, unwanted, unyielding, almost forty years after the war. Because of this, allied forces still stand on this continent. Today, as forty years ago, our armies are here for only one purpose: to protect and defend democracy. The only territories we hold are memorials like this one and graveyards where our heroes rest.

We in America have learned bitter lessons from two world wars. It is better to be here ready to protect the peace, than to take blind shelter across the sea, rushing to respond only after freedom is lost. We've learned that isolationism never was and never will be an acceptable response to tyrannical governments with an expansionist intent. But we try always to be prepared for peace, prepared to deter aggression, prepared to negotiate the reduction of arms, and yes, prepared to reach out again in the spirit of reconciliation. In truth, there is no reconciliation we would welcome more than a reconciliation with the Soviet Union, so, together, we can lessen the risks of war, now and forever.

It's fitting to remember here the great losses also suffered by the Russian people during World War II. Twenty million perished, a terrible price that testifies to all the world the necessity of ending war. I tell you from my heart that we in the United States do not want war. We want to wipe from the face of the earth the terrible weapons that man now has in his hands. And I tell you, we are ready to seize that beachhead. We look for some sign from the Soviet Union that they are willing to move forward, that they share our desire and love for peace, and that they will give up the ways of conquest. There must be a changing there that will allow us to turn our hope into action.

We will pray forever that someday that changing will come. But for now, particularly today, it is good and fitting to renew our commitment to each other, to our freedom, and to the alliance that protects it.

We're bound today by what bound us 40 years ago, the same loyalties, traditions, and beliefs. We're bound by reality. The strength of America's allies is vital to the United States, and the American security guarantee is essential to the continued freedom of Europe's democracies. We were with you then; we're with you now. Your hopes are our hopes, and your destiny is our destiny.

Here, in this place where the West held together, let us make a vow to our dead. Let us show them by our actions that we understand what they died for. Let our actions say to them the words for which Matthew Ridgway listened: "I will not fail thee nor forsake thee."

Strengthened by their courage, heartened by their value, and borne by their memory, let us continue to stand for the ideals for which they lived and died.

Thank you very much, and God bless you all.

我们在这里纪念那历史性的一天，盟军联合作战，为自由而收复这片大陆的日子。

在四年之久的时间里，众多欧洲人生活在恐怖阴影之中，自由国家陷落，犹太人在集中营哭泣，数百万人为自由而哭喊。欧洲被奴役，世界为营救行动而祈祷。在这里，诺曼底，营救行动开始。为了这项人类历史上空前绝后的伟大事业，联军从这里开始奋起反抗暴政。

我们此刻站在这个法国北方海岸人迹罕至、风霜尽吹之地，空气清新。但四十年前的此刻，这里硝烟弥漫，呼声鼎沸，枪林弹雨，炮声隆隆。黎明，1944 年 6 月 6 日那个黎明，225 名突击队员跳下英国登陆艇，冲向这些悬崖峭壁的底端。

这次登陆任务中，他们的使命异常艰巨：攀上这些陡峭荒芜的悬崖，解除敌人的武装。盟军获悉这个滩头装备了高效的杀伤武器，

将用于阻止盟军登陆。

突击队员们仰面看到敌军士兵就在悬崖边，用机枪向他们扫射并投掷手榴弹。美国突击队员开始攀援。他们把绳索投往头顶的悬崖，借此引体向上。一个突击队员倒下，另一个接续上去；一根绳索打断，抓住另一根绳索继续攀援。他们边攀登，边驻足还击。不久，他们一个接一个攀上崖顶。他们夺回悬崖之上坚实土地之时，也是他们夺回欧洲大陆的开始。225名人来到这里，两天的战斗之后，只剩下90名士兵一息尚存。

在我背后是纪念碑，象征那些刺入悬崖顶端突击队员的威力。在我前面是那些投身于此役的人。他们是奥克角之子，他们是战胜悬崖绝壁的勇士，他们是协助解放一个大陆的冠军，他们也是结束一场战争的英雄。先生们，看见你们，我想起了斯蒂芬·斯彭德的诗句，你们是那些人："以命相许你的荣耀谱写了天空的绚丽。"

我想，我知道你们此刻可能在想什么："我们不过是伟大战役的一部分，在那个日子里无人不勇。"是的，无人不勇。你们记得51高地上贝尔·米林的故事吗？四十年前的今天，英国军队被困于一座桥的附近嗷待增援。突然，他们听到了风笛的声音，有人以为他们在做梦。但这不是梦，他们抬起头看见贝尔·米林吹着风笛，带领援兵冒着枪林弹雨，进入他们所在的战地。

劳得·拉瓦特是其中之一。劳得·拉瓦特是苏格兰人。他走向桥的时候平静地宣布："对不起，我来晚了几分钟。"好像他因交通拥挤受阻，其实他刚刚与战友们从血战中的剑滩杀出。

这里有勇猛出奇的波兰人，当入侵开始时投身于敌战区与欧洲最后的自由领土之间，还有已经在这个海岸见识了征战之残酷的大无畏的加拿大人。他们知道在那里等待他们的是什么，但是他们没有退缩。而且一旦越上加诺海滩，他们决不回头。

所有这些人都是一份荣誉花名册的一部分，这份花名册上的名字呼之骄傲而自豪，明亮如他们色彩斑斓的着装：皇家温尼伯突袭队、波兰第二十四骑兵、皇家苏格兰枪手、尖叫之鹰、英格兰义勇军装甲师、法国自由武装、海岸警卫"火柴盒舰队"、还有你们，美国突击队。

自你们参与的那场征战至今，四十个寒暑过去了。拿下这些峭壁时你们正年轻，有些不过初出茅庐，热爱置身其间的生活。但是你们却打包了自己的和平，进入他人的战争。为什么？为什么你们这样做？是什么驱使你们不顾自我保护的本能，冒着生命危险攀登这些峭壁？是什么激励所有到这里集合的军人？望着你们，我们觉得我们知道答案。这个答案就是信心与信仰，就是忠诚与爱。

诺曼底人坚信：在这个滩头阵地或下一个阵地上，他们所战是正义之役，所为是博爱之举，所获将是正义上帝应允他们此战的奇迹。这是一种深深的认知——祈祷上帝我们不要失败——使用武力争取自由和使用武力实行侵略征服，两者在道德上有天壤之别。你们到此是捍卫自由，不是侵略征服。所以，你们和你们的战友们没有怀疑自己的出征理由。你们确信是正确的。

你们都知道有些事值得为之献身。一个人的国家值得为之献身，民主值得为之献身，因为它是最高荣耀的政府形式，由人民设计而成。你们都热爱自由，你们都坚决反对暴政，你们都知道自己国家的人民站在背后支持你们。

那个早晨，在这里参战的美国军人都知道，开战的消息在自己家乡的黑夜中扩散。人们虽然无法确定，但他们心有灵犀。以致于在乔治亚，他们凌晨四点涌入大小教堂；在肯尼亚，他们在自己门

前跪下祈祷；在费城，他们敲响了那座自由钟。

还有一些事帮助了诺曼底登陆日的人们，他们坚信上苍于此事件中将在这里施展其大手笔，而上帝乃是这一伟大事业的盟友。所以，在开战前夜，当沃·武尔顿上校要求他的伞兵部队与他一起跪下祈祷时，他告诉他们："不要低下你的头，而要抬起来，所以你能仰望上帝并要求他为我们的所为祝福。"也是在那天夜里，马修·莱德威将军在他的帆布床上，于黑暗中聆听上帝对约书亚的承诺："我将不使你失败也不会抛弃你。"

正是这些激励了他们，凝聚盟国团结一致。

当战争结束，生活得以重建，政府得以回归人民，新的民族得以诞生。在所有这一切之上，新的和平得以确立。工作繁多，任务艰巨，但是盟国以倒在这里人们的信仰、信心、荣誉和爱凝聚力量，他们共同重建了一个新的欧洲。在那里，在从前的敌人之间（他们都曾承受了如此巨大的痛苦）第一次产生了伟大的和解。美国尽了自己的义务，开创马歇尔计划帮助我们的盟友和我们先前的敌人重建家园。马歇尔计划导致大西洋联盟，伟大的联盟作为我们自由、繁荣与和平的保障延续至今。

无论我们拥有多么伟大的成就与成功，并非战后的一切都令人满意或按照计划进展。一些获得解放的国家失败了，失败的巨大悲哀回荡在华沙、布拉格和东柏林的大街上，渲染了我们的时空。进入这片大陆腹地的苏联军队在和平降临时并未撤离。他们仍然待在那里，未经邀请，不受欢迎，强硬不退，直到战后至今已将近四十年之久。今天，一如四十年前，我们聚集这里只为一个目的：保护和捍卫民主。我们唯一占据的领地是类似这样的纪念地，还有墓地，在那里安息着我们的英雄。

　　在美国，我们从两次世界大战中学到了痛苦的教训。守在这里，枕戈待旦，护卫和平，比丧失自由后再背着挡箭牌冲过大洋，仓促应战要好一些。我们懂得了，针对欲意扩张的残暴政府，孤立主义过去不是而且永远也不会是最恰当的反应。但是我们总是试图准备适应和平、准备阻止侵略、准备谈判以削减军队，而且在内心准备再度追求和解。事实上，没有和解像与苏联和解那样更使我们充满期盼。所以，我们在一起可以减少战争危险，从现在到永远。

　　不应该忘记的是俄国人民在二战期间的巨大损失中承受的痛苦：两千万人死亡，这向全世界表明了结束这场战争所需的骇人听闻的代价。我可以扪心禀告你们：我们美国人不想要战争。我们想从地球上抹去现在持在人类手中可憎的武器。而且让我告诉你们：我们准备好了收复那片失地。我们期待来自苏联的某些迹象：他们愿意向前走的迹象，他们持有与我们相同意愿与爱好和平的迹象，以及他们愿意放弃征服之道的迹象。现实必须有所改变，以便能够使我们将希望付诸实际。

　　我们将恒久地祈祷有朝一日变化的到来。但是现在特别是今天，重申我们彼此之间的、对自由的以及对保护这一自由之联盟的承诺，不仅必要而且正当其时。

　　四十年前的盟谊使我们今天以同样的忠诚、传统和信念连结在一起。我们为现实结盟。美国盟国的意志对于美国至关重大，美国安全的保障对欧洲民主国家的持续自由至关重要。我们过去跟你们站在一起，现在也跟你们站在一起。你们的希望就是我们的希望，你们的命运就是我们的命运。

　　在这里，在这个西方共同守护的地方，让我们向我们的死难者起誓。让我们用自己的行动向他们表白，我们深知他们为何而死。

让我们用行动告诉他们，马修·莱德威听到的那句承诺："我将不使你失败，也不会抛弃你。"

他们的勇气支撑我们，他们的价值激励我们，他们的记忆凝聚我们，为了那些他们生死与之的理想，让我们继续恪尽职守。

非常感谢你们，上帝护佑你们。

第三节 精彩语录

The men of Normandy had faith that what they were doing was right, faith that they fought for all humanity, faith that a just God would grant them mercy on this beachhead, or on the next. It was the deep knowledge—and pray God we have not lost it—that there is a profound moral difference between the use of force for liberation and the use of force for conquest. You were here to liberate, not to conquer, and so you and those others did not doubt your cause. And you were right not to doubt.

诺曼底人坚信：在这个滩头阵地或下一个阵地上，他们所战是正义之役，所为是博爱之举，所获将是正义上帝应允他们此战的奇迹。这是一种深深的认知——祈祷上帝我们不要失败——使用武力争取自由和使用武力实行侵略征服，两者在道德上有天壤之别。你们到此是捍卫自由，不是侵略征服。所以，你们和你们的战友们没有怀疑自己的出征理由。你们确信是正确的。

You all knew that some things are worth dying for. One's country is worth dying for, and democracy is worth dying for, because it's the most deeply honorable form of government ever devised by man. All of you loved liberty. All of you were willing to fight tyranny, and you knew the people of your countries were behind you.

你们都知道有些事值得为之献身。一个人的国家值得为之献身，民主值得为之献身，因为它是最高荣耀的政府形式，由人民设计而成。你们都热爱自由，你们都坚决反对暴政，你们都知道自己国家的人民站在背后支持你们。

When the war was over, there were lives to be rebuilt and governments to be returned to the people. There were nations to be reborn. Above all, there was a new peace to be assured. These were huge and daunting tasks. But the Allies summoned strength from the faith, belief, loyalty, and love of those who fell here. They rebuilt a new Europe together. There was first a great reconciliation among those who had been enemies, all of whom had suffered so greatly. The United States did its part, creating the Marshall Plan to help rebuild our allies and our former enemies. The Marshall Plan led to the Atlantic alliance—a great alliance that serves to this day as our shield for freedom, for prosperity, and for peace.

当战争结束，生活得以重建，政府得以回归人民，新的民族得以诞生。在所有这一切之上，新的和平得以确立。工作繁多，任务艰巨，但是盟国以倒在这里人们的信仰、信心、荣誉和爱凝聚力量，他们共同重建了一个新的欧洲。在那里，在从前的敌人之间（他们都曾承受了如此巨大的痛苦）第一次产生了伟大的和解。美国尽了自己的义务，开创马歇尔计划帮助我们的盟友和我们先前的敌人重建家园。马歇尔计划导致大西洋联盟，伟大的联盟作为我们自由、繁荣与和平的保障延续至今。

Here, in this place where the West held together, let us make a vow to our dead. Let us show them by our actions that we understand what they died for. Let our actions say to them the words for which Matthew Ridgway listened: "I will not fail thee nor forsake thee."

在这里，在这个西方共同守护的地方，让我们向我们的死难者起誓。让我们用自己的行动向他们表白，我们深知他们为何而死。让我们用行动告诉他们，马修·莱德威听到的那句承诺："我将不使你失败，也不会抛弃你。"

Strengthened by their courage, heartened by their value, and borne by their memory, let us continue to stand for the ideals for which they lived and died.

他们的勇气支撑我们，他们的价值激励我们，他们的记忆凝聚我们，为了那些他们生死与之的理想，让我们继续恪尽职守。